CHRISTMAS COUNTDOWN

Alexa Tewkesbury

CWR

Published 2014 by CWR, Waverley Abbey House, Waverley Lane, Farnham, Surrey GU9 8EP, UK. Registered Charity No. 294387. Registered Limited Company No. 1990308.

For a list of National Distributors visit www.cwr.org.uk/distributors

Concept development, editing, design and production by CWR
Printed in the UK by Page Brothers
ISBN: 978-1-78259-144-3

Hi! We're the Topz Gang

We are Topz because we all live at the 'top' of something ... either in houses at the top of the hill, at the top of the flats by the park, even sleeping in a top bunk counts! We are all Christians, and we go to Holly Hill School.

We love Jesus, and try to work out our faith in God in everything we do – at home, at school and with our friends. That means trying to show God's love (especially at Christmas!) to the Dixons Gang who tend to be bullies, and can be a real pain!

If you'd like to know more about us, visit our website at **www.cwr.org.uk/topz** You can read all about us, and how you can get to know and understand the Bible more by reading our *Topz* notes, which are great fun, and written every two months just for you!

> **'You will ... give birth to a son, and you will name him Jesus. He ... will be called the Son of the Most High God.'**
> **(Luke 1 v 31–32)**

Sunday 1 December

7.30am

It's Advent Yay-hay hooray and fantasmagroovers!

(I made that one up, by the way – fantasmagroovers, I think it's going to be my word of the month!) Anyway, as I say, it's Advent. That time when we start to get fantasmagrooverlistically (another one of mine) excited about celebrating Jesus' birthday on planet Earth.

And what makes that countdown to Christmas complete? A fun-stacked, chocolate-packed ADVENT CALENDAR of course!

Mine isn't the same as Sarah's. We tried that one year and it didn't turn out well. Too easy to get confused. We kept eating each other's chocolate! I said it didn't matter as long as we both got a chocolate each for the day, but Sarah said of course it mattered because an Advent calendar's a very personal thing. Mum said perhaps we should each keep our calendars in our own rooms instead of side by side in the living room, and then we'd know whose was whose. Sarah just looked at her and said, 'And how is that helpful? I can't be expected to go to bed in the same room as chocolate and not eat it. There would end up being a one-night chocolate fest and I would have to spend the rest of Advent without a chocolate reindeer or Christmas pudding in sight … And I'm just not ready for that kind of deprivation!'

So this year Sarah's calendar is the same as Josie's, and mine's the same as Paul's. That way we've still all got someone to compare chocolate experiences with when we see each other, but without the confusion factor. Only the thing is, when I got up this morning (especially early so that I could do the whole grand opening of window number one thing and get Advent off to a fantasmagroovers, not to mention yummily chocolatey, start), what did I find? Nothing! That's right. Absolutely diddly-doodly-numbles! Behind that window was nothing but empty space. Now, is that fair? My mouth's been ready for that chocolate since two weeks ago when I bought the calendar.

I said to Mum, 'Do you think it's too early to ring Paul?'

Mum pulled the duvet over her head and said, 'Of course it is! It's Sunday and it's not even 8 o'clock in the morning. They're probably all enjoying an undisturbed lie-in. As I would be doing if I wasn't talking to you!'

'I doubt Paul is,' I said. 'It's the start of Advent calendar day. He's probably been up for ages like me.'

'You'll see him at church in a little while,' Mum said. 'Can't it wait?'

'No!' I said. 'It's a matter of life and death!'

'Is it really?' Mum sighed.

'Well ... it could be,' I said. 'I'm missing a chocolate.'

Mum peeped out from under the duvet. 'John,' she said. 'Go back to bed.'

So here I am. Sitting on my bed. And the lack of chocolate number one is driving me absolutely crackers. You see, is it just number one chocolate that's missing? Or is it worse than that? Supposing number two's not there either? And number three? And number four? Supposing I have bought the one and only chocolate-packed Advent calendar in the whole history of Advent calendars that's NOT PACKED WITH CHOCOLATE?

I'm itching to have a look. Just a sneaky little peek behind window number two. And maybe window number three. A tiny check on the yes there is or no there isn't chocolate situation. But I can't – because today is window number one day and if I break the rules, who knows what might happen? Advent chaos, that's what! So what I really need to ask Paul is whether he found his number one chocolate safely tucked in behind his number one window where it should be, or whether all he got was fresh air, too?

And I really need to know right now … before I can't stand it any longer … and Advent chaos takes over …

'Mum,' I said. 'So do you think it's too early to text him?'

'John!' Mum groaned (always a bad sign). 'Go back to bed.'

8.15am

Texted Paul. Well, it was after 8 o'clock so I figured he'd have to be up by now:

Guess wot?

Unfortunately I then accidentally pressed 'send' too soon so I had to start again. Before I'd finished, my phone rang.

It was Paul.

'What?' he said.

'What?' I answered.

'Exactly – what?' Paul said.

'Erm ... '

'"Guess wot?" WHAT?'

'What? Oh!' I said. 'The text. That wasn't meant to be all of it.'

'All of what?'

'The text.'

'What text?'

'The one I just sent.'

'The one that said "Guess wot?"?'

'Yeah, I pressed "send" too soon.'

'You do that a lot.'

'I know.'

'So anyway, John – WHAT??'

'Well, the thing is, Paul,' I said, 'have you opened your number one window yet?'

'Have I ever!' Paul said.

'And did you find a chocolate?' I asked.

'Of course I did! What did you think I'd find? A tooth?'

'No, it's just ... I didn't get one.'

'What – a tooth?'

'No! A chocolate.'

'What do you mean?' Paul asked.

'I mean, there wasn't a chocolate behind my window number one,' I said. 'And I was just texting you to see if yours was the same.'

'No, sorry,' Paul said. 'I had a lovely bit of chocolate. A Christmas tree. Delicious! And I tell you what, it's put me right in the mood for Advent.'

'Good. Great,' I nodded.

'Weird you didn't get one,' said Paul.

'Weird and annoying,' I agreed.

'Oh, well,' he added cheerfully. 'Better luck tomorrow. But then, of course, Advent's about a lot more than just chocolate, John.'

Paul's right, I know he is. Advent's about way, WAY more than just chocolate. It's a brilliant time – getting ready to celebrate the birth of Jesus! The birth of the SON OF GOD! How could anyone not be excited about that? I love Advent. It's just … well, I reckon even Jesus might have been the teeniest bit disappointed if he'd missed out on a chocolate Christmas tree.

Monday 2 December

7.15am

It's cool. Everyone can relax. There WAS a chocolate behind window number two! And now that I've had my first chocolate Christmas pudding of the year, Advent's starting to feel well and truly … Adventy.

I was going to try to make it last for as long as possible – the chocolate Christmas pudding, that is, not Advent. When I put it in my mouth, I tried to get it under my tongue. Sadly, it popped out and the temptation was too much. Chomped it up in a second. I now can't wait till tomorrow morning when I can open window number three.

But listen to this: Sarah took out her number two chocolate (an angel), put it in an envelope and said she was taking it next door before the school bus came!?!

I said, 'You're doing what?'

She said, 'You heard. You see, John, some of us aren't greedy chocolate guzzlers. Some of us prefer to wait and enjoy our chocolate angels with a really good friend.'

'But, Josie's probably eaten hers already,' I pointed out.

'I'm not talking about Josie,' Sarah replied. 'I'm talking about Mollie. I do have more than one really good friend, you know.'

'Won't Josie be disappointed?' I said.

'Why should she be?' Sarah answered. 'Anyway, Mollie wants to see my

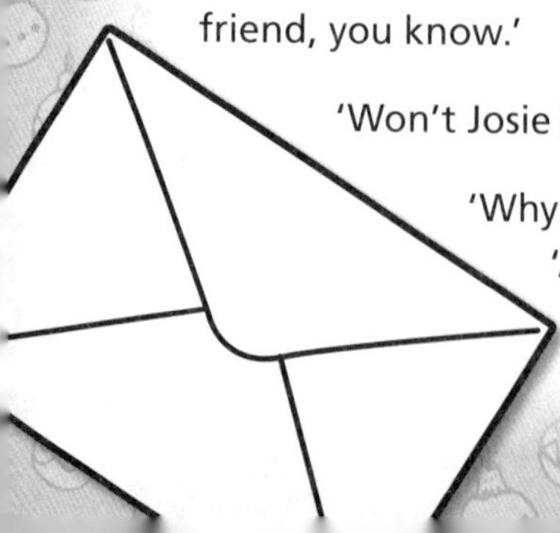

chocolate angel before it gets eaten, plus she wants to show me her super-posh Advent calendar. I want to see it, too. I bet it's loads nicer than ours. Everything Mollie's got is loads nicer than ours.'

And there she goes again, on and on about Mollie McGee. Ever since Mollie McGee and her family moved in next door a few weeks ago, it's been all 'Mollie this' and 'Mollie that'. It's as if nothing else matters to Sarah anymore. I said, 'Well, I'm quite happy with <u>my</u> Advent calendar, thank you very much.'

Mollie Mollie Mollie Mollie Mollie Mollie Mollie Mollie Mollie Mollie

Sarah said, 'I didn't say you weren't. And I'm quite happy with mine.'

'Doesn't sound like it,' I grunted.

Sarah said, 'Oh, you're just jealous because Mollie wants to show me her calendar and not you. Well, it's tough because Mollie and I are extremely good friends now and you're just going to have to get used to it.'

See what I mean? Ugh. Double ugh.

It's not that I've got anything against Mollie. I hardly know her. But now that Sarah keeps going on and on and ON about her, it puts me in a bad mood just hearing her name. I don't even know why Mollie wants to be friends with Sarah. She's way older than us – nearly fourteen, Sarah says. So she's not at Holly Hill Primary. She goes to Bruford Secondary near where the Dixons Gang go to school. I think it might all be to do with fashion or something. Sarah's always on about Mollie's clothes and how she wishes she could dress like her. Last week Mollie gave her one of her scarves. It's pink (yuck) with butterflies on and now Sarah wears it ALL the time – except at school obviously, because that's not allowed. Personally I don't think pink scarves with butterflies should be allowed anywhere.

When she showed Mum, Mum said, 'It's a very pretty scarf, Sarah. Are you sure Mollie wants to give it away?'

'Oh, yes,' said Sarah. 'I didn't ask or anything. Mollie just said it could be the "first of my collection". Mollie's got loads of scarves. She says it's really important to have lots of different ones because they can change an outfit just like that.'

'Just like what?' I asked.

'That!' she said. 'Not that I'd expect you to understand. You know nothing about fashion and there's no point pretending you do.'

'Huh!' I said. 'If knowing about fashion means wearing disgusting pink scarves then I'm glad I know nothing.'

Mum gave me one of her warning looks.

'I'm just saying,' I said. But I went up to my room anyway. It seemed like the safest thing to do.

4.30pm

Apparently I'm not the only one Sarah goes on and on to about Mollie. She's been doing it to Josie, too.

I saw Josie in the cloakroom at morning break.
She looked SO upset.

'Are you all right?' I said.

'Suppose,' she answered.

'What's wrong?' I asked.

'Nothing,' she said.

I hate it when people do that. You know there's something wrong. It's written all over their face that there's something wrong. But when you ask them what is wrong they won't tell you.

'Yeah, but there obviously is,' I said.

'No, there isn't,' Josie answered.

'OK.'

'OK.'

'So … ' I said, trying to sound like I didn't really care, ' … shall I just go away, then?'

And that's when Josie burst into tears.
TEARS! I mean, this is Josie we're talking about.
She hardly ever cries. About anything. For Josie to cry, something really, really bad must be going on.

'I've got a Mars bar in my bag,' I said. 'D'you want half?'

Probably not the most helpful thing I could have said.
She shook her head.

'No, you're right,' I said. 'Half a Mars bar's a bit measly. Have the whole thing.'

She wouldn't even look at me.

I tried again. 'What's wrong, Josie?'

Josie sniffed and said, 'If I tell you, you've got to promise you won't say anything to Sarah.'

'What? Why?'

'You've got to promise,' she insisted. 'If you don't promise then I'm not telling.'

'OK, I promise,' I said. 'Now, what is it?'

Josie pulled out a tissue. Girls always seem to have tissues when they need them, I've noticed.

'You know this girl, Mollie, who lives next door to you?' she said sniffily.

Ugh! Bad mood coming on. 'Yeah. What about her?'

'Well, Sarah and me, we were going to go to the cinema next weekend. I mean, it wasn't definitely definite or anything, but we'd talked about it. Sarah even mentioned it yesterday at Sunday Club. Only ... '

Uh-oh. She looked as if she was going to cry again. Maybe I should just have given her the Mars bar whether she wanted it or not.

' ... Only now she says she's going with Mollie instead.

She said she hoped I didn't mind and everything, but Mollie had asked her to go Christmas shopping with her on Saturday and they were going to go to the cinema after that.'

Now I was cross. I'm so sick of hearing Mollie's name!

'Well, you should have told her you do mind, Josie,' I said. 'It's not fair if she said she was going to go with you.'

Josie sniffed again. 'Like I said, we hadn't actually arranged it. I just sort of thought it was happening. And ... oh, I know it sounds stupid, but I don't think I'm Sarah's best friend anymore. I think she'd rather be best friends with Mollie.'

'That's not true, I know it's not,' I said. 'You two will always be best friends. Sarah just gets over excited about stuff. You know what she's like.'

Josie shrugged. 'I thought I did,' she said. 'Now I'm not so sure. She's always talking about Mollie these days: what Mollie's wearing, what Mollie's doing, what Mollie likes watching on TV. She just seems different. She's changed. It's like she's trying to be something she's not all the time.'

Yeah, I thought. It's like she's trying to **be** Mollie.

6pm
I can't say anything, can I? About Josie being upset. I promised I wouldn't. At least I promised I wouldn't say anything to Sarah.

8pm
Told Mum.

8.10pm
Feel guilty now.

8.15pm
But I still haven't said anything to Sarah, and Josie didn't say I couldn't tell Mum. I just thought that maybe Mum would know what to do. Trouble is Mum was already cross when I mentioned it.

'What is going on between you two?' she said after supper. 'Honestly, John, you've been looking daggers at Sarah ever since you both got home.'

'No, I haven't,' I said.

'Erm, yes, actually you have,' Sarah replied.

'I wasn't talking to you,' I said.

'John, I'm not in the mood!' snapped Mum.

'Neither am I,' said Sarah.

'Well, nor am I, come to that!' I said. 'I think you spend way too much time hanging around Mollie! And if you ask me, you were a lot nicer before she moved in!'

'What's that supposed to mean?' Sarah asked.

'If you don't know, I'm not going to tell you!'

'Well, if you don't tell me, how am I supposed to know?'

'STOP IT!'

Mum can shout really loudly when she wants to.

'I've had more than enough of this. I want a bit of space between the two of you. One of you can go upstairs to your bedroom. Who's it going to be?'

'I don't see why it should be me,' Sarah said. 'I haven't done anything wrong.'

But that was the wrong thing she did. So she was the one who had to go upstairs.

And that's when I told Mum.

'Oh, these girls and their friendships,' she sighed. 'Always a drama going on.'

I shook my head. 'No, Mum. Not with Sarah and Josie. They hardly ever have dramas.'

'Well, I'm sure it's nothing to get in a tizzy about, John. Sarah can go to the cinema with Josie another time. Or perhaps she can ask Josie to go with her and Mollie. I'll have a word with her.'

'No!' I said quickly. 'Josie doesn't want Sarah to know she's upset.'

Mum threw her hands in the air. 'You see, John, there's the problem, right there. Lack of communication. Now, go upstairs and apologise to your sister for saying she used to be nicer.'

'She did used to be nicer,' I mumbled.

'John!'

And up I went.

Wednesday 4 December

5pm
Making a Possible Christmas presents to buy list. It was either that or do my maths homework. I did get my homework out of my bag to look at it, but as soon as I saw the words 'equilateral' and 'triangle', I put it away again.

It's actually quite fun deciding what people might like for Christmas. So far my list looks like this:

Possible Christmas presents to buy

- **Mum: A luxury cruise**
- **Dad: A Ferrari**
- **Sarah: Her own flat (to be honest, this is more for me than for Sarah – then I'd get some peace at home)**
- **Dave: A bicycle shop (complete with bicycles to sell)**

- **Benny: Free pizzas for a year**
- **Josie: A safari trip to Africa**
- **Paul: His own personal computer games library**
- **Danny: His own personal gym**

I think, all in all, as presents go, I'm being pretty generous. At least I would be if I could afford them. Sadly, I checked my moneybox earlier and I can't.

So it looks as though everyone's in for their usual pair of novelty socks and fun pack of Maltesers. Mind you, the socks I found for Dad last year were wicked. They were Rudolph-The-Red-Nosed-Reindeer ones and they had a red bobble on each toe that flashed on and off when you walked. Dad said he could wear them with his sandals so that everyone could enjoy them. Mum said if he did that, she'd move out. He still wears them in bed sometimes though.

8.30pm

Sarah's just got back from guess where? Next door and Mollie McGee. They've been doing each other's hair and nails apparently. Sarah's hair is now all stuck up on the top of her head in a sort of wobbly-looking bun, and every fingernail is painted a different colour.

Mum's not happy. 'Well, your nails look very nice, darling,' she said, 'but you're not allowed to wear nail polish to school, are you? What are you going to do in the morning?'

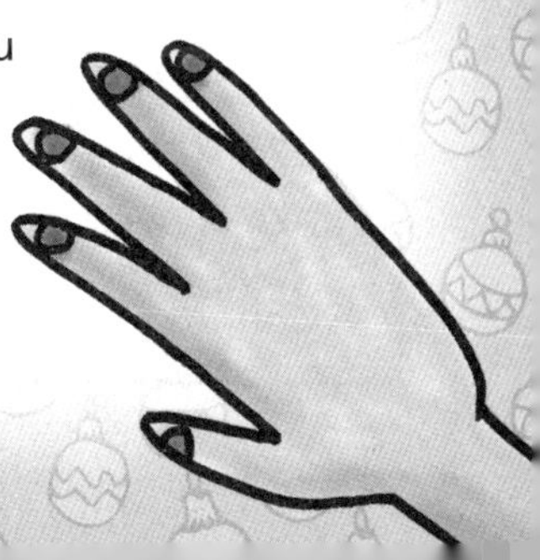

'That's all right,' said Sarah, spreading out her fingers and admiring them in a really annoying way. 'I'll just clean them off with your nail polish remover.'

'Sarah,' said Mum, 'I don't have any nail polish remover. In case you haven't noticed, I don't wear nail polish.'

'Don't know why anyone wears nail polish,' I said. 'I mean, what's wrong with nails being nail-coloured?'

'But everyone has nail polish remover, don't they?' Sarah frowned. 'It's just something ladies have in their beauty bags.'

Beauty bags!?

'Well, not this lady,' muttered Mum. 'In case you haven't noticed that either, I don't even have a beauty bag.'

'Then how am I going to get it off?' Sarah whined.

Mum raised her eyes. 'You'll just have to go back next door and ask if you can use the nail polish remover in Mollie's "beauty bag". I've no doubt Mollie has plenty of the stuff.'

That's when Sarah lost it!

'But I CAN'T! What will Mollie think if she knows we don't even have such a thing as nail polish remover in this house? EVERYONE has nail polish remover in the house! Why does it have to be just us that doesn't?'

Dad did start to argue that he was sure not everyone did keep nail polish remover in the house, but Mum told him not to bother. If he wanted to help, she said, he could drive down to the supermarket and pick up a bottle.

That's where he is now.

'So, do you think I'm right after all?' I said to Mum. 'Do you think Sarah is spending too much time with Mollie McGee?'

Mum gave me one of her withering looks. I decided it was time for bed.

9.30pm
Dad's back. Nail polish remover stinks the house out. How am I supposed to sleep?

9.35pm
In fact how is anyone supposed to sleep?

9.40pm
My sister is polluting the entireness of our airspace.

9.50pm

Dear Lord God, You know it's not like me to moan ... (OK, actually it **is** like me to moan) – But the thing is, I just want my sister back! She's not been the same for weeks now and it's getting worse.

All she seems to want lately is to be like Mollie, and I know that's definitely not what You want. You made each one of us just the way we are and that's how You love us: just the way we are. You don't want us to try to impress each other. You certainly don't want us to try to impress You. And anyway we never could!

Please help Sarah to remember that she doesn't have to try to be something she's not. She doesn't need to be like Mollie. You think she's cool just the way she is.

I want my sister back, Lord. I mean, the old Sarah could be really annoying and there were times when I wished I didn't have a sister at all, but at least she was just Sarah. Now she's trying to be Mollie she's even more annoying! And I'm sure she's starting to care more about what Mollie thinks than about what You think.

Lord God, it's Advent. We're getting ready for Jesus' birthday. The most special and important birthday in the entire history of the whole universe! Sarah's normally really excited about that. Please help her to get excited again. And if she wants to copy anyone, Lord, please show her that the only Person to try to be like today, tomorrow and FOREVER – is Jesus.

10pm

Opening my window. It's really cold. But if it's a choice between being frozen or being suffocated by nail polish remover, I think I'll go with frozen …

'there is nothing that God cannot do.' (Luke 1 v 37)

Thursday 5 December

4.30pm

John's in such a bad mood. He grunted at me in the playground, ignored me in the cloakroom and then pulled a vanishing act at lunchtime.

I found him eventually in a corner of the library. He wasn't reading. He was sitting on a beanbag with his back up against one of the bookcases. Sort of like a bookend.

I said, 'John, I've been looking for you.'

He said, 'Well, fantasmagroovers! You found me.'

I said, 'Why are you pretending to be a bookend?'

He said, 'I'm not.'

I said, 'That's what it looks like.'

He said, 'Only <u>you</u> would think that.'

'No, you actually do look like a bookend,' I said. 'I mean, I'm not saying there's anything wrong with pretending to be a bookend. It's probably quite creative and even useful. Especially if you're propping up really interesting books.'

John looked at me. 'Paul,' he said. 'What do you want?'

I shrugged. 'I just want to know what's up. As my dad would say, you've got a face on like a six-legged octopus.'

'Your dad's quite unusual, isn't he?' John answered.

'Oh, yeah,' I nodded. 'We're quite an unusual family.'

I waited. I thought he'd start to tell me what the problem was. He didn't. He just carried on acting like a bookend.

'It's just not like you to be so ... ' I stopped. I didn't want to make things worse by using the wrong word.

'So what?' John asked.

'Well ... grumpy.'

John glared at me. I'd used the wrong word after all. Everything was worse.

'I don't mean it in a bad way,' I said quickly. 'Everyone has grumpy days. I definitely do. It's just that, when I am grumpy, sometimes it helps to talk about it. You know that old saying – a problem shared is a problem carved.'

'Halved.'

'Sorry?'

'A problem shared is a problem halved.'

'Is it?' I said.

'Yes,' said John. 'Although actually I quite like "carved".'

'Me, too. So, if you want to tell me your problem, we could carve it up together. Right now.'

John sighed. 'I haven't got a problem,' he said. 'I just didn't get any sleep last night.'

'Oh. Why's that?'

''Cos I was freezing cold and the house stunk of nail polish remover.'

'Oh,' I said again. 'Why's that?'

'Well, don't ask me,' John muttered. 'Ask Sarah.'

He got to his feet. I noticed there was a cluster of tiny polystyrene balls clinging to his jumper. They must have escaped from the beanbag. I was about to point them out when he brushed past me. I followed him.

'I'm not sure that's going to work, John. I don't think Sarah's in a very good mood either,' I said. 'She and Josie don't seem to be talking.'

John pushed open the library's swing door.

'Look, Paul,' he said, 'it's really nice of you to want to help and everything, but you can't. And right now? I just want to be on my own.'

He walked off and the door swung closed.

I hate it when there's trouble in Topz.

Friday 6 December

9.30pm
Arrived at youth club in time to hear Greg's announcement: 'Big news, everyone! For those of you coming to Sunday Club this weekend, I shall be making a very special announcement!'

I said to Dave, 'An announcement about an announcement? Who does that? Who makes an announcement about making an announcement?'

'Our youth leader apparently,' said Dave.

'But why?' I said. 'It's cruelty to Sunday Clubbers! Now we're going to spend all weekend until we go to church on Sunday wondering what this "announcement" is going to be.'

'True,' agreed Dave.

I said, 'As if I'm not on tenterhooks enough already with Christmas coming up! We're doing all our decorations at home tomorrow. How am I supposed to concentrate? I mean, for all we know this "announcement" could be bad news.'

'It's probably not bad news,' Dave said. 'If you're going to make a bad news announcement, you probably wouldn't say it was special.'

'Yes, but it could be special to Greg but bad news for us. Greg could be leaving! He could be moving out of Holly Hill – out of England even – to go and work somewhere else ... That'll be it, won't it? In fact, the more I think about it, the worse this announcement could be!'

Dave looked thoughtful. 'I suppose if you put it like that, yeah,' he said.

'What other way is there to put it?'

I couldn't stick it any longer. Not that it <u>had</u> been very long, but I couldn't stick it anyway.

'So, Greg,' I said. 'What's this announcement all about?'

'I'm going to tell you at Sunday Club,' Greg replied.

'Yeah, you could,' I nodded. '<u>Or</u> ... you could just tell me now.'

'No, I can't do that,' he said. 'That wouldn't be fair on the others.'

'Well, don't you think it's just the teeniest bit unfair to announce that you're making an announcement but not until Sunday, and then leave us to go crackers for half the weekend wondering what on earth it could possibly be?'

'Erm ... ' Greg chewed his thumbnail for a moment. 'No,' he said.

9.45pm
I said to Mum, 'You don't think Greg's leaving, do you?'

Mum said, 'Why would I think that?'

I said, 'Because something's going on but he won't tell us till Sunday.'

'Then you'll just have to wait until Sunday, won't you?' Mum said.

I frowned. 'Is that all you've got to say?'

'No, there is something else,' said Mum. 'Night, night.'

11.30pm

So tonight, I'm having John's trouble. I can't sleep a wink. I can't even keep my eyes shut. Every time I close them, they seem to sort of spring open again. It's not even as if I can see anything – partly because it's pretty dark obviously and partly because, even if it wasn't, I don't wear my glasses in bed. Not on purpose anyway. Sometimes I do fall asleep reading and when I wake up, they've managed to slide half way down my nose. One time they did unfortunately slip the whole way down, right off the end and onto the floor. It was Dad who discovered they'd slid off my face – when he came into my room to see why my light was still on. He didn't exactly see my glasses. But he heard the crunch when he trod on them. Mum wasn't happy. I was cool with it, though. I got to miss some school the next morning while we waited for a new pair down at the opticians.

Dad said, 'The answer is always to have a spare pair.'

Mum said, 'No, dear. The answer is always to watch where you're putting your enormous great feet.'

Midnight
Midnight! This is all Greg's fault.

Midnight and a few minutes
No, that's not fair. Some of it's John's fault. He's still got his octopus face on. But today, I think a couple more legs have dropped off.

Midnight and a few more minutes
Going to get a glass of milk. And maybe a biscuit … or six …

Saturday 7 December

9am
Ha! The sleepifying power of milk and biscuits! Dropped off just like that when I lay down again.

And to wake up to, what could be better than a chocolate Advent teddy bear?

10am

I had this idea that today was going to be pretty straightforward. After all, I thought, we're putting up our Christmas decorations. What could go wrong? Dad would get the tree and all the other bits and pieces down from the loft. Mum would get on with writing Christmas cards. It'd be a laugh like it usually is. I was looking forward to having my mind taken off Greg's 'announcement' and John's diminishing number of octopus legs.

Sadly, it's only ten o'clock in the morning and already things aren't going to plan.

We don't have a real tree.

We never usually have a real tree. The tree we put up every Christmas is the fake one Mum and Dad bought before I was born. Only, this year, Dad's decided it would be far more Christmassy to have a real one. Personally, I'm not fussed either way. A tree's a tree, real or not. As long as it's green and you can hang things on it, that makes it Christmassy, doesn't it?

Mum doesn't agree.

'Why go to all the expense of buying another tree when we've got a perfectly good one up in the loft?' she said.

'Because the one in the loft isn't real,' said Dad. 'Not only that, it's past its best. We've had it for years. Last Christmas it looked so lop-sided, I've no idea how that angel managed to stay clinging to the top. And I'm sure it won't be much longer till its little branches start snapping off.'

'Well, until they do,' said Mum, 'there's no need to go out and buy a new one.'

'But think about it,' said Dad. 'We could get a real tree that's a bit bigger. We could have it in a lovely pot on the floor in front of the front window. That way, when we've turned all its lights on, people will be able to see it when they walk by. I love that, don't you?' he added. 'Being able to see other people's Christmas trees all lit up when you walk by?'

Mum folded her arms. 'And what about the needles?' she said.

'What needles?' asked Dad.

'The pine needles that are going to drop off our real Christmas tree all over the carpet! Are you going to hoover them up every day, because I certainly haven't got the time!'

'Not a problem,' beamed Dad. 'You can get Christmas trees that don't drop their needles at all these days.'

'I know,' said Mum. 'They're called "fake". And as it happens, we've got one in the loft.'

11.15am

Mum and Dad finally reached an agreement over coffee and our first mince pies of the Christmassy season. (Not homemade. I think we might be baking next weekend. Mum does the pastry and I put the filling in. In between licking the spoon.)

We seem to be sticking with our fake tree, but Dad said only if he could go out and buy a load of new decorations.

'After all,' he whispered to me, 'the more decorations there are, the less we'll be able to notice the tree.'

Mum seemed quite happy with that. Dad's also going to build a little platform to go under the window that we can stand the tree on so people walking by will see it.

'I don't know,' Mum said. 'Next thing, you'll be wanting to have a special ceremony for turning on the lights!'

'D'you know what?' said Dad. 'That's not a bad idea.'

1.30pm

When Dad said he was going to buy a 'load' of new Christmas decorations, he wasn't kidding. Tinsel, bells, baubles, stars, angels, owls, snowmen, and my personal favourite – candy canes.

When the lady at the Christmas shop was stuffing it all into carrier bags for us, I said, 'Dad, you don't think that maybe you've gone slightly over the top?'

Dad just smiled and said, 'Christmas comes but once a year, Paul. Be prepared, that's my motto. Because next year, when Mum agrees to our having a real and much larger Christmas tree, we'll have plenty of things to hang on it.'

Mmm … It will be interesting to see how that goes …

As we left the Christmas shop, we saw Sarah. She was with a girl who was very tall.

'Hi, Paul!' said Sarah.

'Hi, Sarah!' I replied.

'Been Christmas shopping?' she asked, nodding towards all our carrier bags.

'Well, it's more Dad than me,' I said.

'Christmas decorations,' said Dad. 'You can never have too many, that's what I say.'

I looked at the tall girl.

'This is Mollie,' said Sarah. 'We're doing Christmas shopping, too.'

'Hello,' said Mollie. 'What's your name?'

Sarah didn't give me the chance to answer. 'Sorry, Mollie,' she giggled. 'This is Paul. I keep forgetting you don't know everyone in the Topz Gang.'

'And you must be Paul's dad,' said Mollie to Dad. 'You look so alike.'

I wasn't sure what to make of that. OK, so Dad and I both wear glasses, but I've always thought that that's where the similarity ends. For one thing I'm a lot shorter. WAY shorter. For another I'm years younger. I mean, no offence but Dad's got quite a few lines on his face and a fairly round tummy. What exactly was Mollie trying to say?

'Oh,' I said. 'And you're very ... tall.'

'Mollie's older than us, silly,' smiled Sarah. 'But we're best friends now, aren't we? Mollie lives next door.'

'Best friends?' I asked.

'Yes,' said Mollie. 'In fact, the lady in the shop we were just in thought we were sisters!'

Both girls seemed to find this incredibly funny. Not sure why.

'So, I'll see you tomorrow at Sunday Club, Sarah,' I said.

'Actually, maybe not tomorrow,' Sarah said.

'But you've got to come tomorrow!' I said. 'Greg's making some sort of announcement. Didn't John tell you?'

Sarah shrugged. 'Haven't really seen him today. I've been with Mollie.'

'Oh,' I said. 'But you've got to come. For all we know it could be really bad news.'

'I'm sure it's not,' Sarah answered. 'Anyway I'll be with Mollie again. We are going to spend tomorrow making Christmas cards. Mollie's going to show me how to do potato printing.'

As they walked away, two things struck me:

1. Mollie seemed to figure a huge amount in that conversation.
2. Who in the world makes Christmas cards out of potatoes?

6pm

Dave rang.

He said, 'Emergency Topz meeting in the park. Now.'

I said, 'I knew it. I knew Greg was leaving.'

He said, 'What's this got to do with Greg?'

I said, 'What else could be an emergency?'

He said, 'We need to talk about John. Actually, we need to talk about Sarah. So can you come?'

'Not sure,' I said. 'We're supposed to be doing the Christmas tree.'

'It's really important, Paul,' he said.

'I know. But you have no idea how focused Dad gets about decorations.'

As it turned out, Dad was cool.

He said, 'Not a problem, Paul, my little look-alike.' Ugh. 'While you're having your important meeting at the park, I shall be in my shed building the Christmas tree display platform. But you'd better get a move on so you're back before it's dark.'

Down at the park Dave, Benny and John were sitting on a bench. Gruff was lying on the grass beside them. Looking at John's face, I could tell there were definitely no legs left on his octopus. To be honest, Gruff didn't look too happy either.

'Where's everyone else?' I asked.

'It's just us,' said Dave.

'But I thought it was an emergency.'

'It is. They just couldn't make it.'

How can you not make an emergency?

'So, what is all this?' I asked.

'Sarah, that's what,' John muttered.

'Well,' added Benny, 'and Mollie.'

When Benny said Mollie's name John gave a growl. An actual growl, like Gruff!

'I met Mollie,' I said cheerfully. 'She's very tall. Lives next door to you.'

John looked at me.

'I KNOW where she lives, Paul.'

'The thing is,' said Dave, 'John's worried about Sarah.'

'I'm not worried about her,' John said. 'I just don't know how much longer I can go on living with her!'

'Sounds serious,' I said.

'It is serious. And it's all Mollie's fault.'

'Really?' I said. 'She seemed OK to me. Well, apart from the fact that her eyes obviously need seeing to. She thought I looked like Dad.'

'Yeah, I get that,' replied Dave. 'You sort of do.'

'No!' I said. 'Because I'm a kid and Dad's ... well ... a lot older than that.'

'I know,' nodded Dave, 'but when you get to be the same age as him, you'll probably look identical.'

'Uh – no!' I said again. 'Because when I get to be the same age as him, he'll be OLD!'

John frowned, 'I thought we were talking about Mollie.'

'Doesn't sound like you want to,' I said.

'I don't! But what I can't stand even more is the stink of nail polish remover, and girls getting all squealy over fashion magazines and what's going on with their hair.'

'I know what you mean,' I nodded. 'If Mum looks in the mirror and decides her hair's a disaster, she freaks out. I'm serious. It can put her in a bad mood for a whole day. Sometimes longer.'

'The thing is, though,' said Benny, 'it's just what girls do.'

'Well, it's not what Sarah does!' John snapped. 'Not this much anyway. Since she met Mollie, all she seems to want to do is go shopping. I think shopping's boring unless it's for DVDs or new bits for my bike. But when

I say that to Sarah, she just gives me a look as if she's so much better than me and says, "Well, that's all you know." And now Sarah's not even coming to church tomorrow because she'd rather hang out with Mollie.'

'Yeah, she told me,' I said.

Dave looked at me. 'Doesn't sound much like Sarah, does it?' he said.

'What do you mean, it doesn't sound MUCH like Sarah?' John said. 'It's not like Sarah at all! Sarah doesn't care about nail polish. She cares about animals. And she never misses church. And a few weeks ago she'd have been dying to know what Greg's announcement tomorrow is all about.' Suddenly, he looked even more grumpy. If that's possible. 'And another thing,' he mumbled. 'A few weeks ago her best friend was Josie. NOT Mollie McGee.'

'Mollie McGee,' I repeated. 'Huh. Cool name.'

John glowered at me.

Yes, GLOWERED.

'Anyway,' I said quickly, 'so what's the plan?'

'There isn't one,' said Dave. 'Not yet. That's the whole point of the Topz emergency meeting.'

Silence. Why were they all looking at me ...?

'Oh, I get it,' I grinned. 'You're waiting for me to be brilliant!'

No answer. Perhaps not.

'What do your parents think?' I asked.

John raised his eyes. 'Mum's fed up because she says all we ever do is argue, and Dad says he doesn't want to come home after work to a battlefield every day. But Mum's surprised that Sarah's not coming to church tomorrow, I know she is,' he added. 'She says she doesn't want to make a big thing out of it, though. She says Sarah can be so stubborn and it could only make things worse. Worse? How could they be worse, that's what I'd like to know?'

I nodded. 'We should pray. Here in the park. Right now.'

'I have been praying,' John sulked. 'I've been praying for Sarah really hard.'

'Yes, but now we can all pray for her together,' I said. 'God likes it when we do that. Then He knows we're really serious.'

'And maybe … ' said Dave. He looked at John cautiously. 'Well, maybe we should pray for Mollie, too.'

'Uh – why?' John demanded. 'She's the one who's causing all the trouble.'

'I know,' said Dave. 'But Mollie needs to know about God just as much as everyone else. For all we know, no one else in the whole world is talking to Him about her.'

John looked doubtful. 'I don't think it'll make any difference,' he muttered. 'All Mollie seems to care about is shopping.'

'What do you mean?' I said. 'Prayers ALWAYS make a

difference! It's like the angel says in the Christmas story in the Bible – you know, just after telling Mary that she's going to have a baby and He's going to be God's Son: " … there is nothing that God cannot do."'

'Paul's right,' said Dave, and Benny nodded.

'Thanks very much,' I said.

Dave said, 'God might not always answer prayers the way we expect Him to, John, or the way we want Him to. But He always answers. So prayers always make a difference.'

'[Mary] gave birth to her first son ... and laid him in a manger – there was no room for them to stay in the inn.' (Luke 2 v 7)

DAVE

Sunday 8 December

8am

I'm ready for church. I've been ready for half an hour.

Trouble is, Mum and Dad aren't up. But why would they be? Church doesn't start until half past ten.

Trouble also is, I'm dying to know. It's today – the announcement about The Announcement!

I don't think I'd be dying to know quite so much if it wasn't for Paul. He's gone on and on about it. Then on about it some more!

He's texted this morning already: *Greg leaving? Yes/No.*

I wasn't sure how to answer. Texted back: *No.*

Paul texted again: *How can u kno that???*

I texted back: *Can't.*

Paul texted: *Not helpful.*

I texted: *Sorry.*

9am

It's so weird how sometimes an hour can go r-e-a-l-l-y slowly and other times an hour can go really fast! The last hour's been SO slow, I reckon it's going backwards. I wouldn't be at all surprised if any minute now I didn't find myself brushing my teeth and getting ready for bed – yesterday.

10.10am

Mum just called, 'We're going, Dave! Are you ready? Hurry up or you'll make us late!'

Huh?!

2.30pm

So ... The Announcement.

We all sat down ready for Sunday Club and waited.

In church before we went out, we'd listened to a poem. It was about Jesus' mother, Mary, going on the long journey to Bethlehem with Joseph to be counted for the census. The poem's written as if it's Mary talking. She says how hard it is to have to travel such a long way because she's about to have her baby. She talks about how relieved she is when she and Joseph arrive in Bethlehem. Then she says she could cry when they find there's nowhere for them to stay because the inns in the town are already full of people. All Mary wants is a place where she can have her baby in peace. But there isn't a spare room to be had.

Until they're offered a stable.

It might be dingy and smelly and dirty, but Mary's SO grateful.

'What did you think of the poem?' Greg asked.

The Sunday Clubbers who didn't know about The Announcement nodded and said, 'Yeah, good, liked it.'

The Sunday Clubbers who DID know about The Announcement didn't say anything at all. Why was Greg talking about a poem? What about The Announcement?

'I mean, imagine what it must have been like for Mary to have travelled all that way and end up with nowhere to stay,' Greg continued. 'She's about to have a baby. She would have been exhausted. Joseph must have felt bad, too, realising that he wasn't going to be able to find his wife somewhere comfortable to rest.'

Paul put up his hand. 'Erm … this is all really interesting and everything,' he began. 'And don't get me wrong, I thought it was a really cool poem and Mrs Jackson read it in a really cool way, but … haven't you forgotten something?'

Greg thought for a moment. 'No, I don't think so,' he said.

'The Announcement?' said Paul. 'You said on Friday at youth club that you'd be making "an announcement".'

'Did I?' Greg said. 'Oh, yes, so I did. I'll be coming to that in a bit.'

Paul said, 'Is there any chance you could maybe come to it now, because if you're leaving Holly Hill some of us would just really like to know?'

'Leaving? Who said anything about me leaving?' Greg actually looked confused and it takes a lot to confuse Greg.

I said, 'That's what Paul thought you were going to announce.'

'Did he?' Greg said. 'I see. Well, I'm not. Can we get back to the poem now?'

I glanced at Paul and mouthed, 'Told you.' He looked pleased. But it's still really tricky to concentrate on a poem when you're waiting for 'an announcement'.

'So, there you are, a long way from home and about to give birth to a baby,' Greg continued. 'Not just any baby, mind you, but the Son of God! There's nowhere to stay – and suddenly someone offers you a stable. It may not be the most luxurious accommodation in Bethlehem but at least it gets you inside and off the streets. How are you going to feel now?'

'Relieved,' everyone agreed.

'Just relieved?' said Greg.

'VERY relieved,' everyone said.

Paul leaned towards me. 'Almost as relieved as I'll be when he makes The Announcement,' he whispered.

'Relieved and pretty thankful, I'd have thought,' Greg said. 'Mary is certainly very thankful in the poem. Which,' he added, 'brings me to The Announcement, Paul.'

'Yesss!' Paul said. 'My ears are all ears.'

Greg asked, 'Have you ever stopped to think about how many elderly people there are living in Holly Hill?'

OK so, as announcements go, that's not what I was expecting.

'Erm ... is this still to do with The Announcement?' asked Paul.

Greg ignored the question. 'How many elderly people do you think you know, Paul?' he asked. 'Here in Holly Hill?'

'Not sure,' Paul said. 'A couple. A few. I mean, I know my grandparents really well but they live in Ireland.'

We all answered the same. A couple. A few. Some of the elderly people we knew came to church. Some were neighbours.

'There's a lovely old lady who lives on one side of us,' said John. 'Mrs Allbright. She comes in sometimes to be at home with Sarah and me if Mum and Dad are going out. She found Gruff for me once, too, when he got lost.'

'Think about all those elderly people you know,' Greg continued. 'How many of them live on their own?'

'Mrs Allbright's on her own,' answered John, 'Her husband died.'

'And that's just it,' said Greg. 'Lots of old people have lost their husbands or wives. And they might live a long way from their families. In fact, many elderly people spend most of their time by themselves. We're all so busy with our own lives these days,' he added, 'and in all the hustle and bustle, there must be times when they feel there's no place for them. No room anymore. Christmas will be one of those times. So this Christmas ... ' Greg paused and looked at Paul. 'Are you ready for this, Paul?

Because

this

is

The Announcement.'

'Ready, yeah!' said Paul.

'This Christmas, we're going to make sure that no one elderly and alone in Holly Hill gets forgotten. There isn't going to be "no room in Bethlehem" for those who often have to spend Christmas by themselves. Not this year. We're going to arrange a party for them on Christmas Eve. Right here in the church hall.'

Greg glanced around. 'Now, admittedly it's not the most glamorous place for a party. But then that stable wasn't the most glamorous place for the Son of God to be born in either. And it didn't stop it being the most momentous event. So, Sunday Clubbers, this Christmas Eve it's up to us – **"Operation: Room In The Stable"** has begun.'

Paul leaned towards me again. '"Operation: Room In The Stable" – I like that,' he whispered. 'ORITS. Sounds so much more fun than The Announcement I thought Greg was going to make.'

'It's going to be lots of fun, Paul,' said Greg. Paul's whispers aren't really that much like whispers. 'It's also going to mean a lot to organise – which is where you all come in … '

Tuesday 10 December

5.30pm

Homework. Ugh! As it's this close to Christmas, you'd think teachers would be glad not to have any more marking to do. Wouldn't they rather be doing things like writing Christmas cards and making present lists? Obviously not or they wouldn't still be setting homework. Our teacher must want to spend the last week of term marking a mini-project on bees and honey making.

And what a weird topic for December! I mean, at least if it was polar bears I suppose I could understand it. Then we could draw snow and icebergs and other Christmassy-looking stuff. Instead of which I have just drawn a honeybee on a daisy. And when was the last time you saw that on a Christmas card?

8pm

Josie's had a really good idea for ORITS. She told me at lunchtime. I was supposed to be playing football with John, Benny, Danny

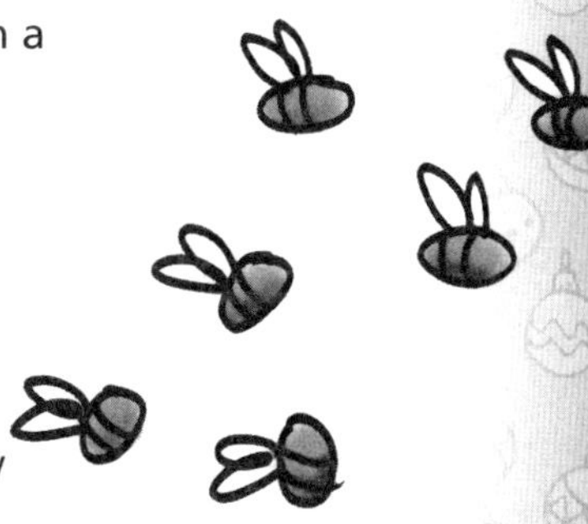

and Paul, but it rained. So we were all stuck inside for another wet playtime.

When Josie found us, we were playing flick football all crouched on the cloakroom floor.

'What are you doing?' Josie asked.

'The thing about living in Britain,' Paul said, 'is that you have to get really creative when it comes to the weather. More often than not it's likely to be raining. Therefore, more often than not, outdoor football will be impossible. So finding an alternative is an absolute must.'

'And you call this an alternative, do you?' Josie said. 'Crawling around on the cloakroom floor?'

'We are not <u>just</u> crawling around on the cloakroom floor,' said Benny. 'We are crawling around on the cloakroom floor whilst playing flick football.'

'Which is?' Josie asked.

'It's where you screw a piece of paper up into a little ball,' John said, as if it was obvious, 'and flick it between you with your fingers.'

'Oh,' said Josie. She didn't look as impressed as we thought she might. 'So you don't have goals or anything like that?'

'There are the goals,' I said, pointing to the two empty lunchboxes we'd placed at each end of the cloakroom. 'As a matter of fact, if you'd come in a few moments earlier, you'd have been in time to see me score.'

'OK,' said Josie. 'Well, as exciting as this is, can I talk to you about ORITS?'

'What? Right now?' I said.

'Yes, please,' Josie answered. 'But you can carry on football-flicking at the same time, if you like.'

Paul looked doubtful. 'Not sure about that,' he said. 'It may look easy to you, Josie, but flick football actually requires a huge amount of concentration. I'm really not sure I could flick the ball at the same time as talking.'

We all sat on the benches.

'So, what's this about ORITS?' I asked.

'Well, I know that the church has already got some money to pay for the party,' Josie said. 'But if we could raise some extra as well, then we'd be able to do a whole lot more. So, what I was thinking was – how about carol singing?'

I nodded. 'Very seasonal,' I said.

John made a face. 'I'm not very good at singing.'

'It doesn't matter,' said Josie. 'With all of Topz together, I think we'll sound great. I bet if we did a bit of door-to-door, and spent some time down at the shopping centre, we could raise quite a lot.'

John made another face. 'When you say "all of Topz together", have you asked Sarah?'

'Well, no,' said Josie. As soon as John mentioned Sarah's name, I didn't think Josie looked quite so excited. 'I was hoping maybe you could. I told her about ORITS but she didn't seem that interested. I don't even know if she'll end up going to the party. When I asked her, she said she wasn't sure and she might be doing something with Mollie.'

John raised his eyes. 'What a surprise.'

'But Sarah did give the invitation to Mrs Allbright, didn't she?' I said.

Greg had asked us all to take a few party invitations to give to any elderly people we knew around Holly Hill who might be on their own over Christmas. He had a long list of people he was going to deliver to as well. John took some, but said he'd give one to Sarah for her to take round to Mrs Allbright. He knew Sarah was really fond of her so he thought she'd want to do that.

John shrugged. 'Dunno if she's taken it or not yet. But she said she would, so I guess she will.'

'So anyway, carol singing,' said Josie. 'What do you think?'

'Great idea,' I said. 'But we should probably practise.'

Paul grinned. 'Yeah. I wonder if people donate money to carol singers who can't sing?'

'Probably,' I said. 'Just to make them go away!'

Josie asked, 'Can I have a go?'

'What at?' I said. 'Bad carol singing?'

'No!' said Josie. 'Flick football.'

The trouble with Josie is that she's not just good at

sport – she's really good at sport (if you can call flick football 'sport'). The five of us had been playing all lunchtime and only managed four goals between us. Josie played for five minutes before the bell rang and scored six all on her own. Argh!

Wednesday 11 December

6pm

Sarah came to carol singing practice at lunchtime.

'Why do you all look so surprised?' she said. 'I like singing carols.'

'Are you going to come to the shopping centre on Saturday?' asked Josie, hopefully. 'We're going to carol sing outside the baker's.'

'Yeah,' said Paul. 'That way we'll be able to smell mince pies at the same time for a double Christmassy effect.'

'Probably,' said Sarah. 'I could ask Mollie to come, too.'

'No, you can't,' said John. 'This is a Topz thing. In any case, Mollie hasn't practised.'

'Yes, John, but Mollie has a really good singing voice,' said Sarah. 'She has proper lessons with a proper singing teacher. In fact, she's thinking of putting herself on YouTube. I told her she should. So if she's singing with us, she's going to make us sound way better.'

'I think we sound pretty good as just Topz,' I said. 'But if Mollie wants to join in, then I guess that's OK.'

John made a face. 'What do you mean "OK"?' he snapped. 'It's not OK with me!'

'The more singers we've got, the better, really,' said Josie quickly.

'Exactly,' said Sarah. 'And the more good singers we've got, the better.'

So anyway, the way things stand with ORITS at the moment, Mollie might come carol singing with us on Saturday. Could be good.

The down side is that we seem to have lost John.

6.30pm

Went home with John after school because he said he felt 'twinless'.

'I said, "Whatless?"'

He said, 'Sarah spends so much time with Mollie these days that it doesn't feel like I've got a twin anymore.'

I said, 'But she used to spend a lot of time with Josie.'

John said, 'Yes, but that's Josie, isn't it? That's different.'

As far as being 'twinless' goes, I wasn't sure that it was.

I said, 'I could come back with you after school, if you like. You can pretend I'm your twin.'

John looked at me. 'No, that's OK. But you can still come back after school.'

John and Sarah have got a real Christmas tree. Their mum and dad don't like fake ones. It's quite big and there are presents under it already.

I said, 'How come you've got presents? It's ages till Christmas.'

He said, 'Mum's got a friend in America. She always sends stuff early. One year everything arrived on bonfire night.'

'Wow,' I said. 'That is early.'

'And quite cruel in some ways,' John said. 'Imagine knowing that there are Christmas presents in the house on 5th November, but having to wait till 25th December before you can open them!'

'Mmm,' I agreed. 'Tough.'

'And Mum never hides them away. She just leaves them out on purpose so we have to look at them every day. She says it's a good lesson for all of us in self-control.'

I decided to be direct.

'John,' I said. 'Please come carol singing with us.'

'No,' he said. 'Not if Mollie's going. Anyway, like I said, I can't sing.'

'I think you sing really well,' I said.

'And how would you know?' he asked.

'Because I often stand next to you in church. Also I'll always remember you as the singing slow worm in that school musical we did in Year 4 about reptiles.'

'That was a weird musical,' John said.

'It was,' I agreed. 'But you were great as the slow worm. So how about it? Please come carol singing.'

John looked at me. I thought he was going to say yes.

'No,' he said.

8pm
Josie rang.

'What are you doing?' she said.

'Homework,' I said. 'Well, sort of homework.'

'Bees?'

'Yeah. Only I got bored with drawing bees on flowers. So instead I've just drawn a bee skiing down a snow-covered leaf wearing a bobble hat. I quite like it.'

'You should give that one in with the project,' said Josie.

'Actually, I was thinking it might make quite a good Christmas card,' I said. 'Be even better if it was one of those musical ones. Dad got one from Nan and Grandad last year. Every time you opened it, it tootled this weird version of "We wish you a merry Christmas". Dad loved it. He'd sit there for ages opening and closing it and making it stop playing at different moments in the tune. Drove Mum mad. Until one day she "accidentally" spilt a cup of coffee all over it. After that all it did was buzz.'

'Shame,' said Josie.

'Not really, after a while it *was* pretty annoying.'

'So anyway, did you manage to persuade John to change his mind about carol singing?' she asked.

'Not yet, no.'

'Oh.'

'But don't worry,' I added quickly. 'I think it's brilliant that Mollie might come, don't you? And I'm sure John will want to be there in the end.'

'*I'm* not,' sighed Josie. 'I'm not sure you understand how much he doesn't like Mollie.'

'I think I do actually. It's just that ORITS isn't about John or Mollie. Or Sarah, come to that. It's about – well – ORITS. And any minute now, John will realise that, I know he will.'

9.30pm

Dad came in to say night-night.

I said, 'Dad, are we putting the Christmas tree up this weekend?'

We have a fake one. Mum and Dad don't like real ones. Sarah and John's looked fantastic, though.

Dad said, 'I think we'd better. Otherwise it'll be time to take it down again and it won't have been up long enough to gather dust. Which reminds me,' he added, 'I hope your nan and grandad send me another one of those musical Christmas cards this year. In fact, I must remember to get one for Mum. She loved it.'

9.45pm

Been reading my Bible. The book of Isaiah. I love that part in chapter 9 that talks about the birth of Jesus: 'He will be called, "Wonderful Counsellor," "Mighty God," "Eternal Father," "Prince of Peace."'

The thing that I can still never quite get my head around is that Jesus, the One with all those names – the One who <u>is</u> all those things – was born on earth on the first Christmas and wants to be my best Friend!

10pm

Lord God, thank You for Christmas. Thank You that the birth of Jesus was all part of Your amazing plan to show us how we could be friends with You again. Your plans are always perfect and the first Christmas happened exactly the way You wanted it to.

You have plans for each one of us, as well. Perfect plans. And although ORITS is Greg's plan, I know You like it because it's about caring for people and making them feel special. It's letting them know that they're not forgotten; that we're going to make room for them in Holly Hill this Christmas.

I think John needs Your help to realise that, Lord. I think he needs to see that some plans are bigger than what we want or don't want, and ORITS is one of those plans. Please work it all out, Lord God. Perfectly.

'There were some shepherds in that part of the country ... An angel of the Lord ... said to them, " ... This very day in David's town your saviour was born – Christ the Lord!"' (Luke 2 v 8–11)

Friday 13 December

6.30am

Love it when that happens! You email someone REALLY late at night or REALLY early in the morning, thinking that the person you've emailed won't read it for hours – and then they email you right back! It's like, 'What is wrong with you? Why aren't you in bed?!' And they're probably thinking the exact same thing!

Whenever I get an email from Gabby, she always uses Auntie Chrissie's email address. I don't know why she still doesn't want one of her own. When Uncle Rich and Auntie Chrissie first fostered her, I suppose she didn't know how long she'd be living with them. Perhaps she didn't want her own address because that would make living with them seem permanent, and it might not be. But she's been with them for ages now and she's so much happier than when I first met her! I'm sure she's going to be staying.

I've been meaning to email her all week about ORITS. So last night I thought I'd set my alarm early so that I could get it done before school.

But I didn't need the alarm in the end. I was awake anyway. And instead of a short and to-the-point sort of email, Gabby ended up with a really long one. She's emailed me quite a long one right back.

Hi Josie.

Question: WHAT ARE YOU DOING UP SO EARLY? It's not even Christmas yet. If this is the time you get up in Advent, whatever time will you get up on Christmas Day? I think you need to ask yourself if it's worth going to bed at all on Christmas Eve?

Come to think of it, you're probably wondering why **I'm** up so early. The answer is I have a cold. A really horrid one. I've been awake most of the night because when I lie down I'm so stuffed up I can't breathe, and when I sit up I can't get to sleep. So I thought that if I'm sitting up and not sleeping then I may as well be sitting up and doing something on the computer. Which is when your email flashed up!

ORITS sounds good! Wish I could come and help with the party. But living many miles from you in the middle of the massively muddy countryside (as I do), I don't suppose it's going to be possible. I shall think of you tomorrow doing your carol singing. I know you say you've practised the carols you've chosen, but if you aren't singing it already, please could you do 'In The Bleak Midwinter'? It's my favourite one. You could dedicate it to me and then maybe my cold would get better!

Who's this Mollie? And you don't say much about Sarah? Is everything OK? You haven't had a fallout, have you? I hope not. I can't imagine it. You two are the MOST **best of friends** I've ever met.

Chrissie doesn't want me to go to school today. She says she'd rather I stayed at home and got better in time for Christmas. I said to her, there's loads of time before Christmas and I've **got** to go to school today. The teachers are putting on a special pantomime this afternoon, just for us – Aladdin. I know! Just the teachers! And **my** teacher, Mr Hughes, is playing Dame Nellie Trotwhistle, so you see even if I had THE PLAGUE I'd still have to go. Wish you could come too. Although I suppose if you did, you'd risk catching all my disgusting germs and taking them back to Holly Hill. And then ORITS might turn into OWTT – Operation: Where's The Tissues?!

Speaking of tissues, afraid I shall have to go. Just used my last one and need to find another box-full. Text me tomorrow with how much money you raise carol singing. And don't forget 'In The Bleak Midwinter'. And email me some stuff about Sarah. Better still, tell Sarah to email me! Haven't heard from her in ages! And don't you two dare have fallen out.

Aaah! Serious tissue emergency going on now.

Bye!

XX Gabby

I always put 'Love Josie' and then add kisses after my name. Gabby never puts 'Love' and sticks her kisses in front of her name. I think she must still be nervous of putting 'Love' – I don't know, in case suddenly I disappear or something. Or stop being her friend. It must be hard to trust people completely when you've been let down. As for the kisses <u>before</u> her name, no idea why she does that. None of my other friends do. I guess it's just part of what makes Gabby special. Auntie Chrissie calls her a one-off.

Emailed back:

> Please get well soon. And make sure you don't sneeze over Mr Hughes. It sounds as if he's got enough problems having to play someone called Dame Nellie Trotwhistle.

I wanted to add that Sarah and I hadn't fallen out. I know it's really important to Gabby that we're best friends. She needs to see that friendships and relationships like that <u>can</u> last.

It's just that right now I can't say it and feel as if it's true. I want to, I really do, but I can't. We haven't quarrelled. We still chat. But this time last year, Sarah and me, we were doing all sorts of Christmassy stuff together, <u>and</u> the year before that, <u>and</u> the year before that. Forever really! And this time this year, we haven't even been Christmas shopping together yet. Sarah seems to be doing almost everything with Mollie. Dave says it's a good thing. He says we <u>should</u> have

lots of different friends. That way, if some of them don't know about Jesus, it gives us the chance to tell them. He's right, I know he is, it's just … I loved having Sarah as my best friend and now that Mollie's around all the time, nothing's quite the same.

5pm

Think I'm getting Gabby's cold. How is this possible? We've only been in touch by email. Is this a new way to transmit bugs? Should I be worried? Should I inform the Prime Minister … ? Or is it just a sore throat because I spent all lunchtime practising carols with Topz? Hope it's that one. I have a serious amount of carol singing to get through tomorrow morning and I can't afford to be germy. Giving youth club a miss.

5.30pm

Sarah rang.

'Hello?' I said.

'Are you getting a **cold**?' she asked.

'I hope not,' I said.

'You do sound very croaky,' she said.

'I know,' I said. 'I think it's because I'm not used to all this singing.'

'Me neither,' said Sarah. 'Mollie's teacher shows her how to do it properly. Singing is all to do with how you breathe apparently. Did you know that? Mollie breathes just right so she never gets a sore throat because of singing.'

'Lucky her,' I said.

Pause.

'Erm ... I was wondering about baking,' Sarah said. 'For the party.'

'There's lots to do,' I answered. 'First we've got to decide what we're going to make. Then, when everyone's replied to the invitations – which they have to do by next Friday so that we know how many people are coming – we're going to make a huge, long shopping list of all the things we need.'

'Sounds fun,' Sarah said. 'Maybe I could help with the list. And the shopping. And the baking, too, if you need people to bake.'

I was so happy! I didn't think Sarah cared!

'Of course! You can help with ALL of it!' I said. 'Greg's expecting ORITS to be a VERY BIG party, which means we'll need loads of mince pies and muffins and sausage rolls and everything else. Paul's mum's already offered to make a massive Christmas cake. Christmas cakes can be a bit specialist, Greg says, but Paul's mum's a fantastic cook so I'm confident her cake will be incredibly specialist ... And, Sarah ... '

There was something I wanted to say but I didn't quite know how to say it.

'Yes?' said Sarah.

'Oh, nothing … I'm just really glad you want to help.'

'Don't be silly! Of course I want to help … And, Josie …'

Weird. It sounded as though Sarah wanted to say something to me, too.

'Yes?' I said.

'Oh, nothing … ' she said. 'I'll see you tomorrow outside the baker's for carol singing, Josie. Mollie's really looking forward to it.'

'Me, too.'

'Hope your croaky throat doesn't turn into a cold.'

'Me, too.'

'Yeah.'

'Oh, by the way, Sarah,' I said. 'Is Mrs Allbright coming to the party?'

'Erm … not sure,' Sarah said.

'But you did give her the invitation?' I said.

'Well, I haven't had time yet, but I will. Anyway it's ages till next Friday if that's the day she has to answer by. I'm bound to have seen her by then. Bye, Josie.'

'Bye, Sarah.'

8.30pm
Benny rang.

'Hello?' I said.

'Are you getting a **cold**?' he asked.

'I hope not,' I said.

'Anyway, why weren't you at youth club?' he said.

'Because I'm not sure if I'm getting a cold,' I said.

'Oh,' he said. 'Well, you'd better not be. We tried to give Greg a carol singing demonstration. We thought it was going OK but then Greg said, "Do you know what your carol singing really needs?" "No," we said. "Girls' voices," he said. So you can't have a cold because you're clearly a very important part of tomorrow's fund-raising mission.'

'Don't worry,' I said. 'I'll be there.'

'Yes, but will you be able to sing?'

'Of course,' I said. 'That's why I didn't come to youth club. So that I could rest my voice.'

Not that it was getting much of a rest. I seemed to have been on the phone for half the evening.

'Did you try "In The Bleak Midwinter"?' I asked.

'Yes,' said Benny.

'How was it? Gabby really wants us to sing that one.'

'Not too good,' Benny said. 'You know how it goes, "In the bleak midwinter frosty wind made moan"?'

'Yes,' I said.

'When we finished, Greg said we sounded a lot like the frosty wind.'

'Oh.'

'I know.'

'Is John coming tomorrow?' I asked.

'Don't know. Is Mollie?'

'Yes,' I said.

'Then John probably won't.'

I said, 'But you'll never guess what, Benny? Sarah rang! She does want to be part of ORITS! She wants to help with making food lists and going shopping and doing baking.'

'Who wouldn't want to do baking?' Benny said. 'That's good, though. So you two are still friends, then?'

'Of course we're still friends!' I croaked. 'Why wouldn't we be?'

8.45pm
Dad said, 'You're popular this evening. Lots of phone calls.'

'I know,' I said.

Dad said, 'Are you getting a cold?'

Ugh.

9.30pm

Mum brought me up a mug of hot honey and lemon.

'Dad says you might be getting a cold,' she said. 'This'll help soothe your throat. You'll need it to be tip-top for tomorrow.'

'Thanks, Mum,' I said. Then, 'I've been thinking about the Christmas story,' I added.

'I'm not surprised,' Mum replied, 'seeing as it's nearly Christmas.'

I said, 'In the Bible, it says that the first people God told about the birth of Jesus were the shepherds. And they were the first people He invited to go to the stable to visit the baby Jesus, too.'

'That's right,' nodded Mum.

'A lot of people were probably surprised about that, weren't they?' I said. 'I mean, Jesus is SO important that you'd think the first people God invited to meet Him would have been very important, too. But they were shepherds. Just ordinary shepherds. And they were probably very poor.'

'Oh, I'm sure they were very poor,' agreed Mum.

'But the thing is, by inviting the shepherds first, what God wanted was to show the world that Jesus was born for everyone. Not just for important people, or rich people, but for <u>everyone</u>. So as far as God was concerned, the shepherds were perfect. Just exactly right.' I paused and took a sip of honey and lemon.

'Soothing?' asked Mum.

'Very,' I said.

Mum said, 'You need to stop talking now and save your voice for tomorrow.'

'I will in a minute,' I said. I was just getting to the good part. 'When we carol sing at the shopping centre, I think we're going to be a bit like the angels.'

'Do you now?' said Mum.

'Well, it makes sense,' I said. 'We'll be singing about Christmas and all sorts of different people will walk by and hear us, and <u>they'll</u> be a bit like the shepherds. They'll be ordinary people doing ordinary Christmas shopping, but they'll be exactly the right people to hear our carols. The carols will remind them of why we have Christmas – that Christmas is all about God's love for us. And then,' I went on, 'when we tell them about the party we're raising money for and why we're doing it, they'll be able to see what God's love <u>means</u>. That EVERYONE matters. EVERYONE is important to Him!'

Mum smiled. 'You've thought about this quite a lot, haven't you?'

'Oh, yes,' I croaked. 'I'm a great thinker.'

Saturday 14 December

8am
Throat still not so good.

Dad gave me a glass of salted water and said, 'Try gargling with this.'

I tried gargling with it.

Nearly choked.

'Thanks, Dad,' I said.

'My pleasure,' he answered.

9am
Rang John.

'Please come carol singing,' I said.

'Have you got a cold?' he asked. (Sigh.)

'We can be God's angels today,' I said, 'and remind people how much God loves them.'

'God's angels?' John said.

'Yes,' I said. 'When we sing.'

John said, 'I most certainly don't sing like an angel.'

I said, 'It doesn't matter. What matters is being there.'

John sighed. 'I just don't think I can stand around all morning listening to Mollie and Sarah talking about clothes shopping.'

'But they won't be talking about clothes shopping, will they?' I said. 'They'll be singing.'

'You can sing about buying clothes as well as talking about it, you know,' John muttered.

'What? "In The Bleak Mid-Season Sale"? I don't think so, John.'

Silence.

'So, are you going to come or not?' I said. 'Remember this isn't for me or for Topz. It's for ORITS. What are you going to do?'

'Huh,' John said. 'I'll think about it.'

3.30pm

Sarah's right. Mollie does have a really good voice. Lots of people stopped to listen to our carol singing, but I think it was mostly because of Mollie.

People joined in, too. Fortunately Greg turned up with lots of carol sheets so he was able to hand them around for those who didn't know the words.

We sang 'In The Bleak Midwinter', just like Gabby asked us to, and some of the people who stopped to listen had requests as well. I don't know how much money we raised. Greg's going to count it all up and let us know at Sunday Club tomorrow. I think it must be quite a lot, though. There seemed to be loads of change in our buckets when it was time to stop.

What was really amazing was that the man who owns the baker's (the shop we were singing in front of –

I suppose that makes him the Head Baker) came out and asked what we were collecting money for. When we told him he said he thought it was a fantastic idea and he would donate **ONE HUNDRED** mince pies to ORITS!

Benny's eyes just about popped out of his head. 'One hundred?!' he said. 'That's sort of like a proper mince pie mountain!'

Then the Head Baker went back inside the shop and came out again a few minutes later with a plateful of mince pies for all of us!

The best thing about the whole morning, though, was that John did come and join in. He made sure he didn't stand anywhere near Sarah and Mollie but he was there.

I said to him, 'I'm glad you came.'

'I'm glad I came, too,' he answered. 'After all, like you said, it's for ORITS. And let's face it, if it hadn't been for my angelic singing voice, the baker might not have donated nearly so many mince pies.'

3.45pm

I wonder if Sarah and Mollie are still out.

I asked them if they wanted to come back here for lunch but Sarah said they might be going ice skating. Something else Mollie is really good at apparently.

And Mollie said, 'Anyway, it sounds as though you've got a bit if a cold, Josie, and I don't want to risk catching it. I'm singing in a concert next weekend.'

It was odd, but just as I was about to go home, Sarah ran up and said, 'I'm really sorry about lunch, Josie. We'll do some stuff together in the holidays, yeah?'

Before I could answer, Mollie called, 'I'm ready to go, Sarah! Are you coming?'

And Sarah went. Just like that.

But I'm not sure that she really wanted to.

8pm

Emailed Gabby:

> Hi!
>
> Sorry I didn't text with how much money we raised. Don't know yet. Greg took the buckets away to count it all. He'll tell us tomorrow at Sunday Club, so I'll let you know then. I think it might be quite a lot. Loads of people stopped to listen and loads more joined in. And the Head Baker from the baker's is giving us one hundred mince pies for ORITS and we don't even know how many people are coming to

the party yet! I think Benny has this idea that, if only ten people show up, that'll be ninety mince pies just for him …

How was Aladdin? Tell me everything! I want to know ALL the details. Must have been so weird watching Dame Nellie Trotwhistle and knowing all the time that she/he is actually the teacher who tells you to be quiet in assembly and work harder at learning your times tables!

By the way, you seem to have given me your cold. How this is possible I am still trying to work out, but I definitely have a cold and the only person I know with one is you! You should try some honey and lemon, which is very soothing, but absolutely do NOT try gargling with salt water, which is not.

By the way, too, don't worry about Sarah and me. We're good. Still the MOST **best of friends** you've ever met!

Love Josie xx

'The shepherds went back, singing praises to God for all they had heard and seen; it had been just as the angel had told them.' (Luke 2 v 20)

BENNY

Monday 16 December

8am

I said to Mum, 'Do I have to go to school this week? Seriously, it's not going to do anything for my education. It's so near to the end of term and I'm sure the teachers only make us go because they have to. For instance, this morning we are watching the dress rehearsal for the Year 1 and 2 Christmas play. Very cute but not likely to learn a lot. Then after lunch, we're doing "general tidying" – I think Danny and I are down to help sort out the PE cupboard. Whoopdedoo. Also this afternoon we are having a quiz on bees. Why? We've just finished a project on bees. We really don't need to do a quiz on them as well. So, as I say, Mum – do I have to go to school this week?'

Mum said, 'It's Monday, Benny. Last day of term's Friday. Go and get yourself ready.'

Sometimes with Mum it's as if I haven't spoken.

4.30pm
I was right. Today at school did nothing for my education. Although Danny and I did find an alarming number of plimsolls in the lost property box in the PE cupboard. Not pairs of plimsolls. Just single plimsolls. Weird.

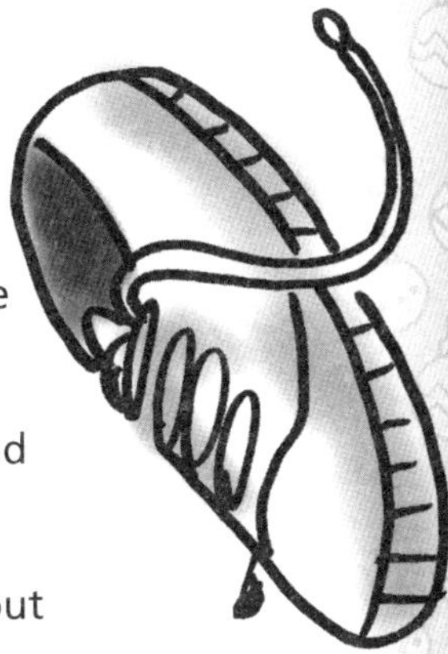

6pm
Saw Greg in the corner shop.

I said, 'Have you had any replies to the ORITS invitations yet?'

Greg said, 'Yes. Thirty-seven so far. And they all want to come to the party!'

'And how many more invitations are out there?' I asked.

'Ooh, hundreds,' Greg said. 'Quite a few anyway.'

'Good thing we raised extra money carol singing,' I said. 'I mean, I know we've got a hundred mince pies, but thirty-seven people amounts to a lot of muffins.'

'Which brings me to entertainment,' Greg said. 'I thought perhaps we could play some games. Unless you and the Gang have got anything else up your sleeves that we could do?'

'Erm ... ' I thought for a moment. 'What about if I do some magic tricks?'

Greg looked impressed. 'Sounds great,' he said. 'I didn't know you could do magic tricks.'

'I don't know if I can either. I've never tried,' I said. 'But how hard can it be?'

'Probably quite hard,' Greg said. 'Anyway, let me know if you come up with anything.'

At least there's a reason to go to school tomorrow now. Lunchtime Topz meeting to talk about ORITS entertainment! Although why wait till tomorrow?

7pm
Rang Danny.

'Danny,' I said, 'can I come round? Some serious ORITS discussion needed.'

'That would be good,' said Danny. 'Sorting out the PE cupboard seems to have switched me into some sort of crazy tidying mode. I can't stop. I've tidied my drawers, my cupboard, and now I'm looking at underneath my bed. Please come and save me before I do something stupid and start to have a clear out under there as well.'

'On my way,' I said.

9pm
When Danny opened the door, he looked worried.

'D'you want to hear something odd?' he said.

'What?' I said.

'I found <u>one</u> plimsoll under my bed,' he answered. 'Not one for each foot which would be normal for me as I have two feet. Just <u>one</u>. It's like the lost property box revisited.'

'That is odd,' I agreed. 'And come to think of it, Mum's always moaning that she can only find one sock of a pair when it comes to hanging up the washing.'

Danny started to look excited. 'It's the same when you're in the car, and suddenly you spot one shoe or one sock by the side of the road! D'you know what I think?'

'No,' I said.

'Aliens!' he said. 'It's the only explanation.'

'Yeah,' I nodded. 'And not just any old aliens. Some alien race with only one leg!'

Once I was inside, we did talk about the possibility of contacting someone with experience in all things outer spacey, but we didn't know anyone. Which was probably just as well because then I remembered we were supposed to be discussing ORITS.

I said, 'Danny, do you know any magic tricks?'

He said, 'I reckon I could make this biscuit disappear.'

I said, 'Go on, then.'

He ate it.

'What do you think?' he said.

'Bit rubbish to be honest,' I replied. Then I made a biscuit disappear, too.

'So,' Danny said, 'what kind of entertainment could we actually do?'

We thought for a bit, then made a list. Here it is:

- **Guitar playing : Danny.**
- **Violin playing : Josie.**
- **Talk on 'Living with a cat like Saucy': Sarah.**
- **Talk on 'Living with a dog like Gruff': John.**
- **Talk on what it's like to be twins: Sarah and John.**
- **Carol singing: could invite Sarah's friend, Mollie. (Check with John.)**
- **Pass-the-parcel: (However old you are you're going to LOVE pass-the-parcel.)**
- **Gymnastics display: (Except Topz can't do gymnastics so maybe not.)**
- **Keepy-uppy display: me, Danny, John, Dave, Paul. Invite audience to join in.**
- **Cookery demonstration: (Although probably won't be room for everyone in church hall kitchen, and anyway, who would cook?)**
- **Joke telling: Me.**

Quite a stonkingly good list, if you ask me. And I bet some of the other Sunday Clubbers will want to do something, too. I reckon Greg's going to be mega impressed! I'm actually quite excited about the idea of telling jokes. I mean, I tell jokes all the time, but I've never done it in public before. Not with a proper audience and everything.

I said to Danny, 'Who knows? This could be the start of my career as a stand-up comedian.'

'Is that what you want to be?' Danny asked. 'A stand-up comedian?'

'It's definitely a possibility,' I said. 'After all, I think you should go with what you're good at and I know I can make people laugh.'

Danny looked doubtful. 'Erm ... yeah,' he said. 'Just maybe not always for the right reasons.'

I wonder what he means?

9.30pm
Went downstairs to say goodnight to Mum and Dad.

'Night, Mum,' I said.

'Night, Benny.'

'Where's Dad?' I asked.

'He's gone to bed,' Mum answered.

'But it's really early,' I said. 'Well, early for Dad.'

'He's not feeling very well,' Mum said. 'Don't disturb him.'

I nodded. 'He's probably got this cold that's going round.'

'I didn't know there was a cold going round,' said Mum.

'Oh, yeah,' I said. 'Josie's had one. She was really croaky. He'll probably be fine in the morning.'

'Yes,' said Mum. 'He probably will.'

Tuesday 17 December

7.30am

I've been looking through my cupboard. If I'm going to be a stand-up comedian for ORITS I should really have a special outfit. A bright yellow suit would be good. Something to make people remember me. Something that would stand out. Sadly, the only yellow things I have in my wardrobe are a pair of broken sunglasses and one scrunched up sock.
Yes, that's right. ONE.

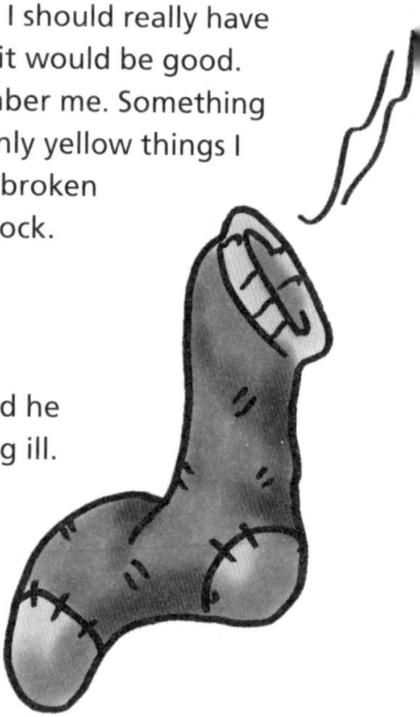

8am

Dad hasn't gone to work. Mum said he was awake a lot in the night feeling ill.

I said, 'If you've got a cold, it can make it hard to breathe.'

Mum said, 'He isn't finding it hard to breathe, and I don't think he's got a cold.'

I said, 'What else could it be? Has he got spots? If he has it could be chicken pox.'

'He hasn't got spots, Benny,' said Mum. 'Now, get a move on or you'll miss the bus.'

'Shall I just say bye to Dad?'

'Best not. I think he might be asleep.'

4.30pm
I took the ORITS entertainment list to school. So far, John and Sarah don't want to give talks, Josie doesn't want to play the violin, none of us want to do gymnastics and nobody's quite sure who would want to watch us cook. Which just leaves Danny playing the guitar, carol singing (although no one mentioned Mollie, not even Sarah), pass-the-parcel, the keepy-uppy demo and joke telling. Personally I think that sounds like a spectacular evening's entertainment, but all anyone else would say was, 'We'd better check with Greg. He might have other ideas.'

I said, 'He hasn't got any other ideas. That's why he asked us to look up our sleeves.'

Even Danny didn't seem that excited, and then he said actually maybe he'd rather not play his guitar.

I love being in Topz and everything but sometimes they're just so …

BORING.

5pm
Rang Greg and read out the entertainment ideas left on the list.

He sounded quite pleased.

'I think the carol singing is a great idea,' he said.

'And so's the keepy-uppy,' I said. 'And the joke telling will be just genius.'

Greg said, 'Let's just concentrate on the carols, shall we, and hold off on the other things for a little while. I mean, they sound fantastic, they really do. But we want to make sure the guests have a wonderful time and carol singing is something I'm pretty confident they'll enjoy.'

Which is obviously Greg-speak for, 'Your jokes are very funny when you tell them to your friends, but I'm not sure you're ready for a proper audience.'

Thanks.

Like I say, **BORING**.

How am I supposed to make the jump from unknown school kid in desperately disgusting school uniform, to dynamic stand-up comedian in memorable yellow suit without a little bit of help from my youth leader? Sometimes life is SO unfair.

6pm
Dad's still in bed. He hasn't been up all day, Mum says. He hasn't eaten anything either.

I said, 'But Dad always eats. And he always goes to work. This is totally un-Dad-like. Don't you think we should ring the doctor?'

Mum shook her head. 'Dad doesn't want me to.'

'You'd ring if it was me,' I said.

'But it's not you, is it?' Mum said. 'Thank goodness. If you weren't eating I'd be really worried.'

Mum was really worried, though. I could tell.

Wednesday 18 December

10pm
It's the first time I've been home all day. Mum says I should go straight to bed and try to get some sleep.

But I don't want to go to bed.

If I go to bed, all I'll do is lie awake and think.

About Dad.

Thursday 19 December

6am
Mum wants me to go round to Danny's. She says it'll be much better for me if I go to school with him and have a normal day – after all, sitting around in hospital isn't the most exciting way to spend your time.

I said, 'Please let me come with you, Mum. I just want to be with Dad.'

She didn't argue with me. She just said, 'OK.' We're going soon.

Time feels so strange when something bad happens.

Dad got taken into hospital in the middle of Tuesday night and I can't believe it's Thursday already. At the same time, it seems like forever ago.

I'll never forget what happened.

When I woke up I thought I was dreaming. I could hear voices and people moving around.

I thought, oh, no! We've got burglars! I need to tell Mum and Dad.

And then my bedroom door opened and I was really scared because I thought it was the burglars and they'd found me!

But it was Mum.

She said, 'Everything's going to be all right, Benny, it really is. But Dad's not very well and the ambulance has come to take him to hospital.'

There were tears in her eyes.

How could she seriously expect me to believe that everything was going to be all right? She was telling me that Dad had to go into hospital and she was crying!

I wanted to run in and see Dad but Mum said no. The people from the ambulance were getting him ready to take to hospital and it would be better not to interrupt them.

'But what's wrong with him?' I said. 'Why does he have to go to hospital anyway?'

Mum sat on the bed. 'They don't know for certain yet,' she said. 'But they think there might be something wrong with his appendix.'

'What's that?' I wanted to know. 'What's a pen … thingy? Is it important?'

'Appendix,' Mum said. 'It's down here,' and she pointed to a place low down on her stomach and a bit to the right.

I felt the place on my own stomach. 'Have I got one? What's wrong with Dad's?'

Mum nodded. 'Everyone's got one,' she said. 'At least everyone who hasn't had it taken out. Sometimes something can go wrong with it, you see. But it's all right. If Dad has to have his appendix taken out, he won't miss it. Not one bit. It's not important at all. Not like your heart or your kidneys or your liver. So you see it's really nothing to worry about.'

'If it's nothing to worry about, Mum,' I said, 'then why are you crying?'

Mum cried properly when I said that. The tears didn't stay in her eyes, they ran all down her cheeks.

'Benny, Dad's really quite ill at the moment, you know,' she said. 'And the chances are he's going to need to have an operation.'

'But he'll be all right?' I said. 'He will be all right, won't he, Mum?'

Mum nodded her head, just a little bit.

'We must pray for him,' she said. 'As much as we can. We must ask God to help Dad get better. We must ask Him to be with the doctors who are going to look after Dad, so that He can guide them and help them find out exactly what's wrong. And we must ask Him to stay beside Dad the whole time. So that he's not frightened.'

Of all the things to pop into my head at that moment, why should it be Christmas? Christmas felt like the least important thing in the whole universe right then. But something in the Christmas story still zapped itself into my mind.

'Mum,' I said. 'God will be with Dad. He won't leave him – not for a second – because He's promised never to leave us on our own, and God only ever tells the truth.'

I reached out and took hold of Mum's hand. 'He told the truth in the Christmas story, didn't He? After the shepherds had visited the baby Jesus, they went off back to their sheep. And they sang their heads off to God because everything had happened just like the angel had told them it would. But all the angel did was give them God's message. And even though it was a properly barmy message (I mean, whoever heard of a king being born in a stable?) it was God telling them what had happened. It was God telling them the truth.'

Mum looked at me. There were still tears on her face but she wasn't crying anymore.

Just then a lady from the ambulance put her head round my door and said they were ready to go. I liked her. She gave me a big smile as soon as she saw me.

Mum told me to throw my clothes on really quickly and we'd follow behind the ambulance in the car.

11am
Mum's gone for a little walk. She says she'll grab a bit of fresh air and maybe a cup of coffee and be right back. She whispered it to me very quietly so as not to wake Dad. We've been sitting by his bed for ages and he's just gone back to sleep.

It must be better for him to be asleep at the moment. The doctors took his appendix out yesterday so he feels really sore where he's had the operation. At least while he's asleep it won't hurt him. Apparently the operation took a bit longer than expected. It was all more complicated to sort out than the doctors thought it would be. But they managed it and now Dad's going to be fine. He'll get better. We're not sure when he'll be able to come home, but he will get better.

So I keep saying it. Over and over again.

Thank You, God. Thank You, thank You.

11.15am

Got a text. It was Greg:

How's ur dad? And how are u?

I texted back: *He's asleep. I'm awake. We're OK. Thanx.*

Greg texted again: *Anything I can do?*

I texted back:

No thanx. All good. Mum says it's times like this she's glad we don't have pets. Only Mum wud think like that.

Greg texted: *Lots of prayers being prayed.*

I texted: *Thanx.*

Then I suddenly remembered ORITS and the entertainment. Texted Greg again.

Not sure I can help with ORITS now. Sorry.

Greg texted: *No worries. Just look after ur dad.*

4pm

Hospitals are really hot. I went to sleep in the chair next to Dad's bed. In the middle of the day. I never go to sleep in the middle of the day.

Dad said, 'I think you and Mum should go home for a bit. You must be worn out.'

I said, 'I'm not. I'm really not. It's just SO hot.'

Dad said, 'Just for a few hours. You can come back again this evening.'

Mum said, 'It's probably a good idea, Benny. It'll give Dad a bit of peace, too.'

Dad winked at me. I couldn't believe it. He was well enough to wink!

10pm
Topz are the best.

Just the absolute, full-on, unbelievably-deevably, STONKING BEST!

We went back to the hospital this evening to see Dad again for a little while before he needed to get some more sleep, and when we got home – THIS!

Danny came round with loads of stuff for us all!

There were three cards signed by Greg and all of the Topz Gang. One was for Dad, one for Mum and one for me.

There were chocolates, too, for all three of us. There was a box of mince pies for me, with the message, 'In case you miss the ORITS party, at least you won't miss the mince pies!' There were two car magazines for Dad to read so that he wouldn't get bored while he was in hospital. And there were two pot plants – one for us to take to Dad in hospital and one for us to have at home. They're amazing. They've got green leaves but they've got what look like red leaves as well. Mum says they're called poinsettias.

I said, 'They're called what-what-ias?'

'P-O-I-N-S-E-T-T-I-A-S,' she said, and she spelt it out for me. 'They're around a lot at Christmas.'

I mean, what a cool word! And what mega cool presents!

I opened my card. It said:

TO BENNY

We're so sorry that your dad's not very well. Hope he gets better soon. Can't wait to have you back doing Topz stuff again. We miss your jokes!

Lots of love,

Dave, Paul, Danny, Josie, Sarah, John, Greg, Saucy and Gruff

At the bottom Greg had written a Bible verse:

'Don't be afraid or discouraged, for I, the Lord your God, am with you wherever you go.' (Joshua 1 v 9)

It was like hearing God speak to me all over again!

When I told Dad how that verse from the Christmas story had popped into my head just when he was going into hospital – about everything happening just as the angel had said it would – Dad said, 'That'll be God. He talks to us like that sometimes. When He wants us to know something, or remember something, He just drops it into our heads.'

I love my dad. I love my mum.

And I love God. He's spoken to me. He's promised to be with me and all of us. Not just at Christmas, but every single day.

And I believe Him. Because God always tells the truth.

'"Where is the baby born to be the king of the Jews? We saw his star when it came up in the east, and we have come to worship him." ... what joy was theirs! [The star] went ahead of them until it stopped over the place where the child was.' (Matthew 2 v 2,10)

DANNY

Friday 20 December

7.30am

LAST DAY OF TERM!

This is good news for so many reasons:

- Two and a half weeks of getting up when I want.
- Two and a half weeks of no homework.
- Two and a half weeks of not having to wear school uniform.
- Two and a half weeks of doing (just about) whatever I feel like whenever I feel like it.
- Loads of Topz time.
- Christmas is nearly here!

I guess we won't be seeing so much of Benny this holiday. His dad's still in hospital. He might not be coming home until Monday. Maybe even Tuesday – which is Christmas Eve. Benny's worried he won't be home in time for Christmas Day.

I said, 'Don't worry, Benny-Benns. Christmas Day is Christmas Day wherever you are.'

Benny said, 'Yeah, but it'll be weird. In any case Dad wants to come home. And to be honest I'm not sure how much longer I can keep heating up! I'm telling you,' he said, 'it's so hot in that hospital it must be just about tropical. Any minute now, Dad's going to use the bathroom and find a crocodile in there! Plus heat makes me sleepy. I don't want to be sleepy on Christmas Day.'

So this is what I've decided: in honour of Benny and his dad, I'm going to persuade Greg to let us do a keepy-uppy display at the ORITS party. After all, it was Benny's idea, and I think it would show him how much we care about what's happened to his dad. I won't tell him till I know we're definitely doing it. But if we all practise really hard at lunchtime then we can show Greg tonight at Youth Club. He probably doesn't realise how awesome we look together, bouncing footballs up and down on our knees. We do, though. We really do! And we could take it in turns so that when one person drops the ball, the next is ready to run on and keep it going. We could even do a line of us at the end, all keepy-uppying together.

And we could do it to music!

The more I think about this, the better it gets!

8am

Been keepy-uppying in my bedroom. Probably not the best place. Bit out of practice.

I knocked my alarm clock off my bedside table. It seems to have stopped ticking.

Mum said, 'What was that noise? I hope you haven't broken something.'

I said, 'Well ... I sort of ... might have. But all in a very good cause.'

Oops.

4.30pm

So there we were. Me, John, Paul and Dave in the playground at lunchtime. Our knees were going up and down like the clappers! The record number of keepy-uppies was twenty-five! (That was me.) Dave managed twenty, John eighteen and Paul twelve, which he says is a personal best!

I said, 'See? We're ace at this! And after today, we've still got three more days to practise. This is going to be the highlight of ORITS.'

Josie and Sarah turned up. 'What's going to be the highlight of ORITS?' Josie asked.

'Keepy-uppy,' I said.

Josie asked, 'Can I have a go?'

''Course. We're practising for the party,' I said.

Josie managed twenty like Dave. We were dead impressed.

'Well, as I'm not playing the violin,' Josie said, 'maybe I could join you guys doing this instead.'

'That's not fair,' said Sarah. 'You'll all be doing something together, and what will I be doing?'

'You could have a go at keepy-uppy, too,' suggested Josie.

'But I can't do it, can I?' Sarah answered. 'It just makes me look silly.'

'No probs,' I said. 'You'll be leading the carol singing. That's really important.'

'Mmm, about that,' Sarah nodded. 'I don't want to do it on my own. Actually, I was thinking of asking Mollie to help out.'

'Why?' said John. 'We don't need her. Besides, ORITS is a Sunday Club thing and Mollie doesn't come to Sunday Club.'

'Yes, but because of Mollie,' Sarah argued, 'we raised loads more money carol singing last weekend than we would have done if it was just us.'

'You don't know that,' said John. 'We might have made exactly the same amount. More, even. She's not that good at singing.'

'She sort of is, John,' said Josie.

'There's no "sort of" about it,' said Sarah.

I said, 'Look, I don't even know if Greg will go for a keepy-uppy display. I just thought it would be cool for Benny to know we were doing it because it was his idea. And, Sarah, I reckon you'll be stonking at leading the carols but you won't be doing it on your own, even if you don't ask Mollie. We'll all be up the front singing with you.'

Then Josie said, 'I'm not bothered about the keepy-uppy, Sarah. I won't do it if it makes you feel left out.'

Sarah looked cross, but I don't think she was cross. I think she was upset.

'I'm not bothered about the keepy-uppy either, Josie,' she said. 'Do what you want.'

And she stomped off.

I felt sorry for Josie. She looked sad.

9pm

Yesss!

The keepy-uppy demo IS ON!

I told Greg at youth club that we wanted to do it for Benny, and when we showed him he loved it. Paul even managed sixteen! I said we could do it to music and everything. So Greg said he'd get hold of the theme tune for Match Of The Day! He also says that, after they've watched us, he could ask the guests if any of them would like a go. That was Benny's idea, too. And so that Benny won't have to miss any of it, Greg's going to video the whole thing! Even Benny's dad will be able to see it. Cool!

Less cool by loads is that it's just going to be the boys. Josie says she definitely doesn't want to join in now.

'But you SO should!' I told her.

She said, 'I don't want to leave Sarah sitting out on her own. She's right. It wouldn't be fair.'

As I say, less cool by loads.

On the plus side, today was the closing date for everyone to answer their ORITS invitations. Greg's counted them all up and there are <u>seventy-two</u> people coming to the party! SEVENTY-TWO!!

Whoop-whoop!

9.45pm
John rang.

'What is it with girls?' He wasn't happy. 'Greg says that on Monday morning we're doing all the food shopping for the party, doesn't he? So that on Monday afternoon, we can do all the baking. So guess what Sarah says?'

I had no idea, but I had a feeling it wasn't good.

John said, 'Sarah says, "It's such a shame Greg's doing everything on Monday. I won't be here. I'm going to London for the day with Mollie and her mum."'

'Since when?' I asked.

'That's exactly what I said,' said John. 'But Sarah just said, "Since ages, actually, and I don't have to tell you about everything I'm doing with Mollie – especially as all you do is get in a bad mood."'

'Erm ... ' I said. 'I suppose she does have a point.'

'No, she doesn't!' John said. 'She must have known we'd be getting ready for ORITS on Monday. When else were we going to do it? I said to her, "But ORITS is so much more important than going to London," and she just said it wasn't her fault. Mollie had invited her out and that was that. "Anyway, I'll be there for the actual party," she said. "Yeah!" I said. "After we've done all the work."'

'And what did she say to that?' I said.

'Nothing,' John moaned. 'She didn't get the chance. Mum said if we didn't stop arguing right there and then, she'd cancel Christmas.'

10pm

I'm kind of with John and Sarah's mum on the arguing thing. I hate it. Topz hasn't felt right for weeks. John and Sarah are either snapping at each other or not talking at all. And one or other of them is always grumpy.

Sarah's just not joining in with us like she used to – which basically sucks.

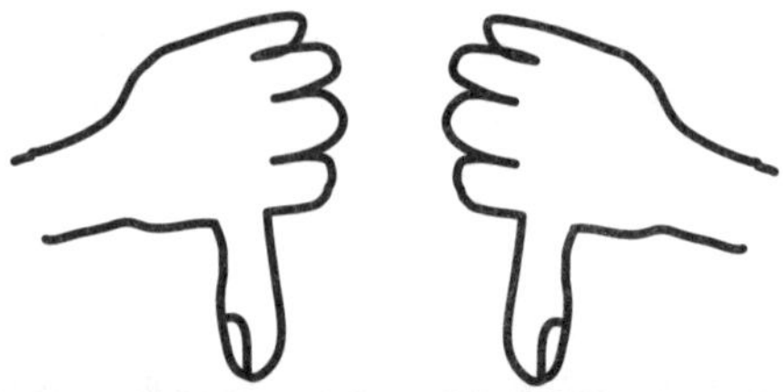

Saturday 21 December

11.30am

Met Paul in the park early for a bit more keepy-uppy practice.

Paul said, 'I wish I was as good at this as you are. I think the main reason I drop the ball more often than you do is because of the length of my legs. They're shorter than yours. Quite a lot shorter. That means the ball has further to fall before it hits my knees because I can't get them up as high as you do. I'm sure that's what makes it harder to control.'

'Maybe,' I nodded. 'I tell you what else is hard to control. John and Sarah's arguing.'

'I know,' agreed Paul. 'It's been going on for weeks.'

'Weeks and weeks,' I said. 'I just want it to stop. I want Topz to get back to normal.'

'Me, too,' agreed Paul. 'Trouble is, John thinks that Sarah's got it all wrong, and Sarah thinks that John's got it all wrong. And unless one of them says sorry, it could go on like that forever.'

11.45am

Lord God, I hate arguments, but You hate them even more. You want us to try to get on with each other; to care about each other and help each other. We can't do that if we're angry all the time. John and Sarah usually fall out and then they're OK again. It's just what they do.

They're brother and sister – I guess that's what happens. But this time it's been going on for ages. So long I can't even remember when it started – or figure out who's right. All I know is Topz feels messed up and Benny's dad has been really ill and it's nearly Christmas and when are John and Sarah EVER going to sort themselves out?

D'You know what it feels like, Lord? It feels like they've both forgotten about You.

When it's Christmas night, I always hope there won't be any clouds. That's because the last thing I do before I get into bed and go to sleep is to look out of my window at the stars. You can't do that if it's all cloudy obviously. I try to imagine what it must have been like being one of the shepherds who's invited to go and see the baby Jesus. There I am looking after my sheep, and suddenly the sky is full of angels and they shine so brightly, all the stars seem to disappear!

Then I think about the star the wise men followed; the star that led them to Jesus. It must have been bigger and more glittery than all the other stars in the sky! The wise men knew that star was special. They knew it meant that Jesus had been born. So they followed it. They didn't argue about following it or worry about following it – they JUST FOLLOWED IT. And it led them all the way to Jesus.

Jesus is like that star. He's bigger and more glittery than anyone or anything else! You gave Him to us! He's there for us to follow, and when we do, He leads us to You. All we have to do is to live the way He teaches us to in the Bible. Then we can be friends with You. **Best** friends forever and ever. And You can help us to live Your way. The **best** way.

Lord God, please help Sarah and John to stop arguing. Help them to remember the Christmas star. Help them to think about Jesus and how special He is. Your Son!

Then help them to stop being grumpy - and JUST FOLLOW HIM!

6pm
I've done something bad. I didn't mean to. I couldn't help it.

I was with Dave and Paul in the skateboard park. We were having a great time until the Dixons Gang turned up. They started kicking a football at us when we skated down the ramps. They do it to each other all the time. Target practice they call it. And I suppose if you don't mind being smacked into by a football when you're trying to skateboard, it doesn't matter.

But we did mind.

So we left.

One of Dixons, Rick, yelled after us, 'Where are you going? You've spoilt our game!'

I wanted to yell back, 'Yeah? Well, you've spoilt ours!'

But I didn't. It's best not to say anything to Dixons. Not when they're all together like that. You only end up in an argument and you know before you start that you'll never win.

So instead, we took our skateboards and went and sat on the bench outside the baker's. It was Paul's idea. He said he wanted to deep-breathe the smell of mince pies again.

We'd hardly been there any time when John walked past with Gruff. I say 'walked'. I think 'was dragged in a completely out-of-control and hilarious-type manner' describes it better. Gruff was pulling like a train!

John just about managed to stop when he saw us, but Gruff kept on yanking at the lead.

'I don't know what's wrong with him today,' John said. He sounded cross. 'He won't stop sniffing. Whatever he's tracking, it must at least be a dinosaur to be this interesting!'

'We haven't seen any dinosaurs,' said Paul. 'But I suppose we haven't been here very long.'

John shook his head. 'Some days Gruff's just like this,' he said. 'Impossible. I think I'll go home. He's wearing me out and my arms must be twice as long as they were when we left.'

We tried to tie Gruff's lead round one of the legs on the bench so that John could sit down and smell the mince pies with us for a bit. It didn't work. Gruff was too excited and wouldn't stay still for long enough.

'He probably knows it's nearly Christmas,' said Dave. 'Have you bought him a present?'

'Yeah,' said John. 'A special dog …' He mouthed the last bit: '… Christmas stocking.'

'That's incredible!' said Paul. 'If you'd said that out loud, would Gruff really have understood?'

'He understands lots of things,' John said. 'D'you want

a walk? Biscuit? Time for supper? Where's the ball? He just has trouble with stuff like, "Stop pulling me, you're yanking my arms out of their sockets!"'

None of us saw Sarah and Mollie. Except Gruff.

He suddenly launched himself at Sarah while John wasn't looking.

John got jerked backwards and fell over.

Sarah lost her balance trying to avoid John and fell on top of him.

The lead got tangled around Mollie's legs and she toppled over, ending up sandwiched between Gruff and a litterbin.

I didn't mean to laugh. I tried not to. I really did.

But it happened anyway. And once I'd started, I couldn't stop. Neither could Dave. Paul laughed so much he slipped right off the bench – which made us laugh all the more.

Sarah was bright red when she got up and Mollie couldn't get up at all with the lead wrapped round her legs.

John tried to untangle it but Sarah just shouted at him. 'How could you be so stupid! Look what you've done!'

Some people stared. Others tried to pretend they hadn't seen what had happened, but we knew they had. It was such a kerfuffle you couldn't miss it.

7pm

I rang John.

'I'm sorry I laughed at you,' I said. 'It just looked so funny.'

'I bet it did,' said John. 'Wish I'd seen it. Rather than being underneath it.'

'Is Sarah speaking to you yet?' I asked.

'Nope,' John said. 'Except to tell me that Mollie fell on her wrist which she could easily have sprained so then she would have been in agony for the whole of Christmas.'

'It wasn't your fault,' I said. 'It was Gruff.'

'I know that,' said John, 'but try telling Sarah. She thinks I did it on purpose. She thinks I do everything on purpose.'

'Fancy some keepy-uppy practice in the park after church tomorrow?' I said. 'Could be our last chance before the party.'

'Yeah,' said John. 'Shall I bring Gruff?'

'Erm ... '

Sunday 22 December

4pm

Sarah was at Sunday Club.

She came up to Dave and Paul and me and said, 'I can't believe what you did yesterday. I thought one day maybe Mollie might want to come to church with me. That she might want to do things with Topz. But you laughed at her. So I don't suppose she ever will now.'

8.30pm

Benny rang.

'Stonking news!' he said. 'Dad's probably coming home tomorrow! Not just in time for Christmas – in time for Christmas Eve as well!'

'Cool,' I said. 'So you won't have to worry about crocodiles at Christmas after all.'

'Looks like it,' said Benny.

'Cool,' I said again.

'What's new?' Benny asked.

I told him about the Gruff incident in the shopping centre and what Sarah had said this morning.

'If it makes you feel any better,' Benny said, 'I'd have laughed, too.'

'Thanks,' I said. 'It was pretty hilarious.'

9.30pm

Benny wanted me to play guitar when we were making the ORITS entertainment list but I said no. I don't really like playing in front of anyone. But then at Sunday Club, Greg said he could do with some musicians to play for the carol singing, so I thought perhaps I should give it a go.

Unfortunately, I've never played Christmas carols on my guitar before. This was clear when I tried to strum along to 'O Little Town Of Bethlehem'.

'What does this sound like?' I asked Dad.

Dad listened. 'Do I get any clues?' he asked.

'Isn't it obvious?' I said.

He shrugged.

'OK,' I sighed. 'It's a Christmas carol and it's about a place.'

He thought for a moment. '"Away In A Manger"?' he asked.

'That's not a place,' I said.

'Yes, it is,' he answered. 'It's the place where Mary laid the baby Jesus.'

On second thoughts, I think I'll stick to keepy-uppy.

10pm

Texted Sarah:

Sorry.

Wonder if she'll text back?

> **'The light shines in the darkness, and the darkness has never put it out.' (John 1 v 5)**

SARAH

Sunday 22 December

10.05pm
Danny just texted. He says he's sorry. I should probably text back. Maybe later.

I wish everything with Topz hadn't gone wrong.

10.15pm
Have to be ready to go to London with Mollie and her mum by eight o'clock tomorrow morning. Mollie's mum's picking me up and we're driving to the station so we can get the train at 8.30am. I think I've sorted everything. I've put out what I'm going to wear. My money-box money is now in my purse and my purse is in my bag. My hairbrush is also in my bag. Mollie says you should never go anywhere without your hairbrush. I'll need to use it in the morning before we go, but I'm worried that I'll forget it if I don't put it in there now.

I'm getting really excited! We'll see all the Christmas lights and Mollie says the shops are full of decorations, too. I'm going to love it, I know I am.

It's just … I wish I was going with Josie.

Monday 23 December

6am

Needn't have worried I wouldn't wake up in time. I've been awake for ages. Typical.

It's weird how much louder my clock ticks when everyone else is asleep. I know it can't be ticking louder. It's just that in the daytime I hardly seem to notice it and right now it's all I can hear. Apart from Saucy's teeny little breathing sounds. She's curled up on my pillow with her nose almost in my ear. I keep prodding her but she won't wake up. Although I think she might be pretending. Maybe she's cross with me because I'm not at home as much as I used to be. I suppose I am round at Mollie's quite a lot now.

But it doesn't mean I love Saucy any less. In fact sometimes I go round to Mollie's and I don't even feel like it. I wish it could just be me in my room with Saucy. I can't say that to Mollie, though. She wouldn't understand.

Mollie says I shouldn't have Saucy in my bedroom and I certainly shouldn't let her sleep on my bed.

I said to her, 'But Saucy always sleeps on my bed. On my pillow actually. I can't stop her doing it now. She'd think I didn't love her anymore.'

Mollie made a face and said, 'You let your cat sleep on your pillow?'

I said, 'Saucy likes to snuggle.'

'Well, I definitely shan't be coming to a sleepover in your room,' Mollie said.

We laughed. Only I'm not sure why because Mollie meant it.

I don't talk to her about Saucy now. I don't think she really likes cats.

She did ask me a few days ago, 'Have you stopped Saucy coming in your room yet?'

I didn't know if she'd be annoyed if I said no, so I didn't say anything. I pretended I didn't hear and talked about something else.

6.45am
I think I'm ready. Apart from eating breakfast and I'm not sure I want any.

I checked my bag. My brush is back in it, and I've swapped purses now, too. Instead of my normal one, I've put my money in the felt one that Josie gave me for my birthday. She made it from a kit. It's purple with a big daisy on the front. I've never wanted to use it in case it got spoilt, but I'll bring it with me just for today. I want to because it was a special present from my special friend and I'll take huge care of it.

And I'll be able to tell Josie I took her beautiful purse with me to London. That'll make her happy.

7am

I hope Josie knows she's still my best friend. I've not really been treating her like that so I wouldn't be surprised if she'd gone off me – if she didn't want to be friends at all anymore. Perhaps that's why she wanted to do the keepy-uppy demonstration with the boys for ORITS. Maybe she thought she'd rather do that than something with me.

I don't know how it's all ended up like this.

When Mollie first moved in next door, I was really excited. She has loads of clothes – really gorgeous tops and skirts and dresses – and she knows lots about how to do hair and make-up. She's got tonnes of what she calls 'accessories', too – bags and scarves and belts and necklaces and bangles, and pretty slides to go in her hair. And when she wanted to be friends, I was so happy! She lent me things. Not actual clothes, obviously, because she's older than me and taller and most of them wouldn't fit, but she was really happy for me to borrow her accessories. She said, 'I'll turn you into a fashion queen if it's the last thing I do!'

Wow, I thought, brilliant! I've always wanted to be fashionable!

I've always wanted to be someone like Mollie!

Then this odd thing happened. All of a sudden – I don't know why – being in Topz didn't seem so interesting. And being best friends with Josie seemed a bit – well – dull. Josie doesn't care about clothes and stuff, and I just wanted to be friends with someone who did.

But the thing about Mollie is – even though she doesn't mind sharing her accessories, what she doesn't seem to like sharing is her friends.

When we go shopping, she always wants to go on our own. I used to ask if Josie could come, but Mollie always said, 'It's better if it's just us. We know what shops we like.'

If we go to the cinema, she doesn't want Josie to come with us there either. The same with going to London today. In fact, whatever we do, Mollie just wants it to be her and me. And she doesn't like it when I go to church or youth club. She says, 'Why do you want to do that? There are so many more exciting things we could be doing together.'

I had this idea that if Mollie got to know Josie and the other Topz, she might want to be friends with all of us. That's why I asked her to do the carol-singing at the shopping centre. I knew she'd like it if I asked her because she's always going on about wanting to be a singer and how her teacher reckons she'll be good enough one day. But I thought that if she spent some time with Topz, she might even want to come to church.

I've tried to tell her about God and how He wants to be her friend but she just laughs at me and says I'm funny and could I please stop going on about it. So all that's happened is that I've ended up not going to youth club every week like I used to do. And some weeks I haven't gone to church either. It didn't seem to matter first of all. I mean, I don't have to go to church every week, do I? It doesn't make any difference to being friends with God, does it?

But now I think, maybe it does. It's as if everything's got in a muddle. All out of focus. Being friends with Mollie seems to have pushed everything else out of the way. Even God.

And I don't see how she'll ever want to come to church now. Not after we all fell over in the shopping centre. If only Paul and Dave and Danny hadn't laughed. I wish SO much they hadn't.

7.15am

And I wish SO much John wouldn't keep saying, 'Why are you always trying to be like Mollie? You're not Mollie, you're Sarah. At least you used to be.'

I'm still Sarah.

I want to be Sarah. It's just that I seem to have got myself all wrapped up with someone else and now … I don't know how to get out of it.

7.20am
Just remembered. ORITS shopping and cooking day today. I bet that's going to be loads of fun. I wish we were going to London some other time.

7.45am
Mum said, 'Have you got everything?'

'I think so,' I said.

'Aren't you the lucky one?' Mum said. 'I wish someone was taking me off to London for the day.'

I nodded.

'And maybe when you get back,' Mum added, giving me one of her meaningful looks, 'you and John might make up and we'll have an end to all this arguing in time for Christmas.'

I nodded again. I didn't know what to say. I hate the arguing, too. It's just that with Mollie, you sort of have to do what she wants, otherwise she doesn't like it. But if I said that to Mum I don't know if she'd understand. And John would think I was silly.

So I haven't mentioned it. I haven't told anyone.

8am
Uh-oh. Doorbell. Time to go ...

9pm
Phew! Days out in London are really tiring! We walked miles! The shops are huge compared to Holly Hill and some of them have ENORMOUS

Christmas trees. And the Christmas lights are gorgeous and so colourful! It was nearly dark when we left to catch the train home, so I saw them all twinkling and shining.

Mollie did so much shopping! Some was for herself and some was for presents. In one shop she said could I go for a little walk with her mum because she wanted to buy something for me and I mustn't see. I felt bad then for not wanting to be there. Mollie and her mum were being so kind. London was amazing all lit up and Christmassy.

But I couldn't help it. Topz were baking and I wanted to be baking with them.

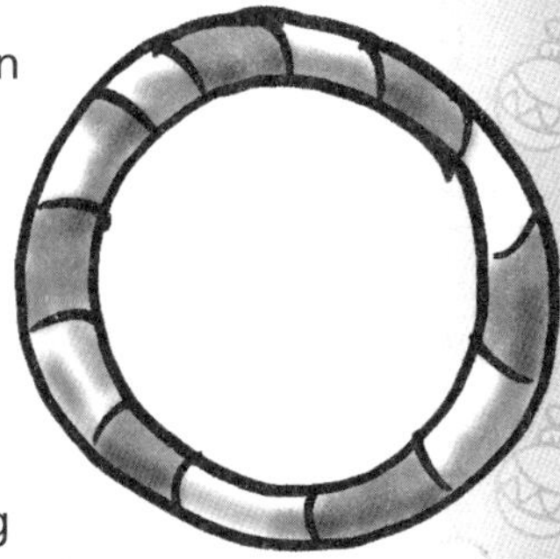

I told a lie, too. I saw a pretty wooden bangle painted all different colours and I wanted to buy it for Josie. Only I didn't think Mollie would like it if I did. So I told her I was buying it for me. The trouble was, Mollie said I should wear it now. Right there and then. So I had to take it out of its bag where the lady in the shop had put it, all wrapped up in tissue paper, and put it on. I hoped I wouldn't knock it or scratch it. I hoped I could wrap it up again like the lady did. I didn't want to wear it at all. I wanted to keep it perfect for Josie.

When we got home, I said bye to Mollie and her mum and thank you so much for a lovely day and I hope you have a very happy Christmas.

But Mollie said, 'Don't be silly. I'll see you before Christmas Day. You should come round tomorrow and help me wrap all my presents. I've got some gorgeous wrapping paper – gold with silver stars. You can use some for anything you want to wrap, too.'

'Erm … ' I said.

'Come for about 11am,' Mollie said. 'Then we can have hot chocolate with marshmallows, too.'

'It's just … ' I tried again.

'What?'

'I don't think I can come tomorrow,' I said quietly. 'It's the party, remember? The ORITS party?'

'I thought that was in the afternoon,' said Mollie. 'You can come round in the morning.'

'But … I need to help get the hall ready in the morning,' I said. 'They were doing all the baking today and I didn't help with any of that.'

'Too right!' laughed Mollie. 'You got to do something much more fun!'

'Yes,' I said.

I'd been planning to ask Mollie if she wanted to help lead the carols at the party. But I hadn't done it yet. I didn't think she would in any case – not after the laughing thing had happened in the shopping centre. Now I didn't even want to ask. I wanted it to be just Topz.

'So, are you coming or not?' Mollie demanded.

Mollie's mum said, 'It sounds as if Sarah's going to be a bit busy tomorrow. But don't worry. There'll be plenty of time to get together after Christmas.'

'But if I don't see you tomorrow, when am I going to give you your presents?' Mollie said.

She wasn't smiling anymore. She looked annoyed. I hate that look.

'Well,' I said, 'I could maybe come in tomorrow after the party. Just for five minutes. I could give you your present then, too. And I could tell you how it all went.'

Mollie grunted, 'Huh! Like I care!'

'Mollie!' said her mum. She sounded cross. 'Anyway, it's too chilly to hang around out here. I'm glad you enjoyed yourself today, Sarah. I'm sure we'll see you at some point over Christmas.'

Mollie looked as if she wanted to say something else, but she didn't. Not even goodbye. She just followed after her mum.

You see? It's impossible.

If you don't do what Mollie wants – everything's just IMPOSSIBLE!

9.30pm

Wrote a text to Josie.

London not nearly so much fun without u. Sorry about everything. Hope we're still best friends. xx

But I deleted it. Instead I texted:

Fab day in London! Took ur purse! See u tomorrow! xx

I waited but she didn't text back.

Maybe she didn't have her phone on.

Maybe it wasn't in the same room.

Sometimes Josie can't even remember where she's put it! She's hopeless when it comes to her phone – really hopeless.

That's why she hasn't texted back.

Yeah, that'll be it.

Tuesday 24th December – CHRISTMAS EVE

8am

Just eaten my last Advent calendar chocolate. It was a star. I was going to text Josie to see if she'd eaten hers, too, but she still hasn't texted me back from last night so I thought I wouldn't. She might not want another text from me.

9am

John is way too excited. He came down to breakfast singing 'We Wish You A Merry Christmas' and he was still singing it, nearly an hour later.

I said, 'What time do we have to be at the hall to get ready for ORITS?'

'Does that mean you're actually coming to help?' he asked.

'That's why I'm asking what time,' I said. 'Why do you have to be so mean?'

Mum banged her mug on the table. A mini wave of tea splashed out of the top.

'It's Christmas Eve!' she said. 'Don't you two DARE start quarrelling again.'

'Sorry,' I said – which was the right thing to say. 'But John started it!' – which wasn't.

'ENOUGH!' Mum shouted. 'Go to your rooms, the pair of you!'

'That was your fault,' John muttered at me as we traipsed up the stairs.

'Well, you shouldn't keep having a go at me!' I hissed. 'You don't know anything about anything!'

I slammed my bedroom door and a load of my Christmas cards fell down.

They're still on the floor now. I can't be bothered to pick them up.

This feels like the **worst Christmas Eve ever**.

10.30am
Mum knocked on my door.

'John's off to the church hall. Are you going with him?'

I shrugged. He didn't want me to, that was obvious. Probably none of Topz wanted me to. I may as well go round to Mollie's and wrap presents. Except she's mad at me, as well.

Mum sat on the bed next to me.

'What is it, Sarah?' she asked. 'This isn't like you. What's happened? What can I do?'

I wanted to tell her. So much. But I didn't know how. If I tried to explain it would all sound silly.

'There's nothing,' I said.

'Off you go and get ready for your party, then,' said Mum. 'You'll feel better for a bit of Topz time.'

Will I?

I wonder …

8.30pm
John says it doesn't matter. He says forgetting stuff

is the easiest thing in the world. Especially when your head's already full up.

'And your head's been full up with Mollie for ages, Sarah,' he said. 'You should have emptied it out a bit and told us.'

I should have done. I know that now. I should have told John and Topz and Mum how possessive Mollie is. How she doesn't want me to have any other friends, how she gets cross if I say no to her. I should have told them I didn't know how to handle it on my own. I should have asked them to help me.

It's just that sometimes talking about things seems much harder than not talking about them.

But because I've been so wrapped up with Mollie, now I've done something really awful. How could I have forgotten something SO important?

Happy Christmas

We put all the tables out in the hall. We covered them in paper tablecloths with a holly leaf pattern around the edges. We put out all the knives and spoons and glasses and jugs and serviettes and Christmas crackers. We hung balloons and streamers here, there and everywhere. Greg had even bought a big, shiny 'Happy Christmas' banner. It looked fantastic. The whole hall did. And that was before we'd even put out the food!

There were plates and plates of cakes and biscuits that Topz had baked with Greg yesterday. There were all the mince pies that the baker had donated, plus sandwiches and sausage rolls, too. And cut up into little squares was a Christmas cake that Paul's mum had made.

Now all we had to do was to wait for everyone to arrive.

The church minibus was out picking guests up, and quite a few people from church had offered to drive anyone else who needed a lift to the hall and back home again afterwards.

As the party guests arrived there was music, and Greg stood by the door with a long list of names. He ticked them off as the different people walked in.

At last he announced: 'That's everyone. Let's get this party started!'

But then John went over to him and said, 'No, wait a minute. Mrs Allbright isn't here yet.'

Greg looked at his piece of paper. 'She can't be coming,' he said. 'She's not on the list.'

And that's when I remembered.

Mrs Allbright wasn't coming – because Mrs Allbright didn't know there was a party.

I hadn't given her the invitation.

John looked at me. It felt like everyone was looking at me. Like everyone knew I was the one who hadn't invited her. Mrs Allbright was going to be on her own at Christmas and I hadn't let her know about ORITS. I'd forgotten.

I felt my cheeks getting hot and my eyes starting to burn. I would have burst into tears right there and then – right in front of everyone – if Greg hadn't said, 'Right, then, Sarah, let's go and make sure the tea urn's on.'

But we didn't check the tea urn. We went to Greg's office instead. He said he was very sorry that he couldn't have a proper chat till the party was over. But he said I could stay in his office if I wanted. Until I felt better.

And that's what I did.

When I went back out to the hall, everyone looked happy. They were laughing and chatting and enjoying the food. Enjoying the company. Enjoying the fact that this Christmas time, they weren't on their own because Greg had made sure there was plenty of room for everyone 'in the stable'.

Everyone except our neighbour, Mrs Allbright. I'd shut her out in the cold. A few times I'd meant to go round and see her with the invitation. But then Mollie had rung or texted and I hadn't done it.

Until in the end I just forgot.

Now it was too late.

Greg took me into his office again after the party. I told him I hadn't given Mrs Allbright the invitation. I told him why. I told him all about Mollie.

Greg was kind. He's always kind and he always understands.

He said, 'Everyone makes mistakes. Everyone gets things wrong. And we can all find ourselves in situations that are difficult to handle on our own. That's why it's so important to talk to someone you trust if you feel things are getting on top of you. We all need help sometimes, Sarah.

'And just remember,' he added. 'Christmas is about light. God's light coming into the world with the birth of Jesus. Whatever happens, nothing can ever separate us from that light – God's love. Because when we believe in Jesus and say we're sorry, God will always forgive us for the things we do wrong.

'The Bible says: **"The light shines in the darkness, and the darkness has never put it out."** That's because the darkness never can put it out. God's love is forever.'

9.15pm

Mum came into my room with a mug of hot chocolate.

'Last hot chocolate before Christmas,' she said.

'Thanks,' I said.

'Are you excited about tomorrow?' she asked.

'Yes,' I said. 'Are you?'

'Excited? Me? Of course I am,' smiled Mum. 'I love Christmas.' She put her arm round me. 'And you're not to worry about Mollie anymore. We'll sort it out. I just wish you'd told us before. Keep praying for her, though, Sarah,' she added. 'God wants to be friends with Mollie as much as He wants to be friends with you and John and all of us.'

9.30pm
Josie texted.

I hope ur OK. So glad Greg told us about u and Mollie. I wish u'd said. I understand now. Please tell me what's going on with u. I'll always try 2 help. Ur my best friend Sarah. Happy Christmas. xx

'A child is born to us! A son is given to us!' (Isaiah 9 v 6)

GRUFF

CHRISTMAS DAY (apparently)

It's early. *Very* early. I know this because it's *very* dark. And I'm still *very* sleepy. Usually I'm the one who has to wake John. I have a range of special techniques for this:

1. Sit on the floor beside John's bed and whine softly and pathetically. If this doesn't work, I move quickly on to number 2.
2. Whine louder. No luck with the whining? I try number 3.
3. Get up on my hind legs and sniff noisily around John's ear. Nothing? Then it's number 4.
4. Sniff ear and whine loudly at the same time. If there's still no movement, the drastic measures of number 5 are called for.
5. Leap heavily onto bed, preferably on top of John, and begin rapid face licking. This always works a treat.

You see, the way I see it, night-time is for sleeping – morning-time is for getting up as quickly as possible and going for a walk before having another snooze. That's how I live my life. That's how I try to persuade John to live his life, too.

So today, I am somewhat confused. It's too early to be morning. Therefore I am still in my night-time sleep mode.

Why then are John and Sarah creeping about and giggling before the sun is even the tiniest bit up?

Is there something going on I should know about???

I have a feeling it could be to do with that rather large tree that appeared downstairs a few weeks ago. Something else I find confusing. I know that humans are very fond of having plants and flowers in their houses, and I can see why. But trees? And in this case a tree that they've hung with all sorts of shiny stuff.

Mmm … All very odd if you ask me.

Odder still, I have the strangest feeling that all of this has happened before. Possibly even this time last year. It's just a bit fuzzy. Last year was … well … a whole year ago. I don't have the best of memories for things past. Live for the moment, that's what I say!

I suppose I shouldn't complain. It's been a very long time since I heard Sarah and John giggling together.

Bickering, yes, but not giggling. Something's been up since that new girl moved in next door. Mollie, they call her. I don't think she likes me very much. She doesn't seem keen on Saucy either. One day Mollie was standing on the doorstep and Sarah asked her to come inside. But she wouldn't. She said, 'No, thanks. Your house is a bit hairy for me. All those dirty animals. Honestly, Sarah, I don't know how you can stand it.'

The cheek of it! Dirty, indeed! I remember thinking, it's a good job Saucy didn't hear that. Saucy is a 'model of cleanliness' (her words, not mine). It's true, though. She spends more time on personal grooming than most dogs do on breathing!

What I didn't realise was that Saucy had heard – which wasn't good news because no one insults Saucy and gets away with it. Before Sarah could grab her, she'd run to the front door, mewing madly, and rubbed herself all over Mollie's ankles.

'Eew! Get it off!' the girl shrieked.

Sarah pulled Saucy away.

'Look at my tights now!' Mollie moaned. 'They're covered in hair. This could be very bad for my singing voice, you know!'

Another moment of confusion. (I have them often.)

What have hairy tights got to do with singing?

Saucy reminded me about allergies. Humans can have allergies to many things: nuts, wheat, milk, pet hair, to name but a few. All I can say is, I'm glad I'm a dog. In fact, the only thing I'd like more than being a dog right at this present moment is to be a sleeping dog.

Not much chance of that, though …

'Are you awake, Gruff?' John is crouching beside me. I have my eyes closed but I can 'sense' him.

'Oh, come on, Gruff,' John whispers. 'I know you're not really asleep.'

This is all the wrong way round. I have a feeling that perhaps John is getting me back for all the times I've woken him up. I half expect he might leap on me in a moment and start licking my face!

There's a giggle. Sarah's here, too. What is going on?

Slowly, I open one eye.

SHOCK!

I am nose-to-nose with a CREATURE!

I leap to my feet, hackles hackling! Teeth … teething! What do I do? Do I run? Do I stay and risk all to protect my masters?

Of course, that's when I realise it's all a HUGE joke. Yes, ha-de ha ha ha.

The other 'creature' is in fact Saucy. It's just that when I opened my one eye she was so close to my face that, half asleep as I was, she looked like a monster.

Not entirely fair. My techniques for waking John have never included scaring him with monsters. Not even not-really-monsters-at-all like Saucy.

'I knew you were awake,' laughs John. Sarah's in fits, too, and Saucy looks immensely pleased with herself.

Oh, yes. What a tremendously hilarious way to start the day when it's not even time for it to start. I give a 'harumph' to show that I'm not pleased. My 'harumphs' are very expressive.

'Here.' John is holding something out towards me. It's all wrapped up in interesting looking paper. 'Happy Christmas, Gruff.'

I look at the parcel suspiciously. (After the whole monster episode, who wouldn't be suspicious?) I stretch my neck and let my nose do a little investigating ...

That's when I discover – it's edible! This is a parcel of **FOOD!**

I snatch it out of John's hands. I don't mean to snatch. Sometimes the smell of food just has that effect on me.

I drop it and glance up at John.

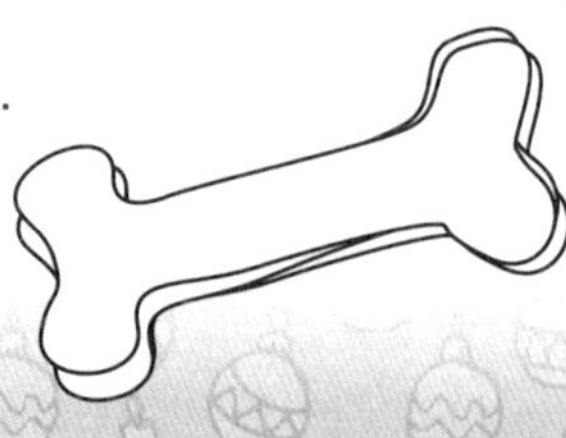

'It's OK, you can open it,' John says. 'It's your Christmas present, silly.'

I have very sharp teeth. The opening takes only a moment. In seconds I'm munching away on a crunchy biscuit bone … In even fewer seconds, it's gone.

Sarah laughs. 'It's a good job that's not your only present, Gruff.'

You mean there are OTHER presents? Perhaps this getting up before the crack of dawn is more fun than I thought.

John gives the top of my head a scratch, then he and Sarah disappear downstairs.

Licking my lips, I glance at Saucy.

'I didn't really think you were a monster,' I say coolly.

'No,' purrs Saucy. 'Of course you didn't.'

'Anyway, what is all this?' I ask. 'Why the presents? Is it my birthday? No one told me it was my birthday. If I'm going to be another whole year older, I'd quite like a bit of warning.'

Saucy raises her eyebrows – as much as a cat can anyway. 'Don't tell me you've forgotten what day it is?'

I think for a moment. 'Erm … yes, I have.'

'It's Christmas!' says Saucy.

'Christmas,' I repeat. 'Yes, that's what John's been saying. And Christmas would be … ?'

Saucy's tail flicks backwards and forwards impatiently.

This is obviously something I should know.

'Christmas would be Jesus' birthday!' Saucy meows. 'Don't you dogs know anything?'

I hate it when Saucy does that. Dogs know lots as it happens, for example:

- the best places to bury bones and much-loved toys.
- the best trees and lampposts to find the sniffiest sniffs.
- the quickest way to get a strange cat out of the garden.
- how to look hungry enough to get a human to share their biscuits with them.

What do cats know? How to wash. That's about it really.

'OK,' I say. 'Well, if you're so clever and it's Jesus' birthday, how come I'm the one getting the presents?'

Saucy raises her eyes and stretches, her pointy claws digging into the carpet.

'That's how humans celebrate Christmas,' she says. 'They put up decorations, give each other presents, eat special food and spend time together. But,' she added, sitting up and scratching an ear, 'Sarah says that what God wants is for them to remember Jesus, too: that He was born in a stable in Bethlehem to bring peace and happiness to the whole world. She says that people had done so many wrong things, they weren't close to God anymore. So God sent Jesus to show everyone how to be friends with Him again.'

All right, so maybe Saucy knows a little bit more than just how to wash.

'It's all coming back to me now,' I say. 'So, this Christmas thing – it happens every year?'

'Yes!' says Saucy. 'Year after year after year!'

Interesting, I think. And super-dooper.

'Well, happy Christmas, Saucy,' I say. I'm tempted to give her a lick as a sign of affection, but last time I did that she hissed at me and said I had bad breath.

'Happy Christmas to you, too, Gruff,' Saucy says.

I yawn. 'I suppose that's why John and Sarah are up so early. Excited about presents. Do you think that means they're friends again?' I ask. 'I hope they are. I don't think John's ever taken me for so many grumpy walks.'

Saucy purrs and curls up beside me. 'I hope so, too,' she says.

> **'The people who walked in darkness have seen a great light. They lived in a land of shadows, but now light is shining on them.' (Isaiah 9 v 2)**

SAUCY

CHRISTMAS DAY

I can always tell when Sarah's not quite herself. She doesn't have to say anything. There's just something about the way she cuddles me. She gets a sad look in her eyes, too, and she sighs.

Today she's excited. More excited than I've known her for ages. And she and John seem to be getting along fine – much to everyone's relief, it has to be said.

But she's still not 'right'. I caught her sighing in the lounge before they all went off to church. It's at times like this, I wish I could say, 'Come along, Sarah. Sit yourself down and tell me all about it.' As it is, the best I can do is wrap myself around her legs and purr like an engine.

Just now she's very busy. She and her dad are helping out in the kitchen.

'All systems go!' I heard her mum say when they got home about half an hour ago. They've been peeling and chopping and stirring ever since.

Gruff's not here. John's taken him for a walk. Probably just as well. When Gruff gets excited the best place for him is out of the house. Once he'd properly cottoned on to the fact that it's Christmas Day, there was no calming him down. He didn't give me a minute's peace while everyone was out at church.

'Let's see who's fastest up and down the stairs!' he said.

'No!' I said.

'Let's have an obstacle race round the lounge!' he said.

'No!' I said.

'Let's see who's the first to catch their own tail!' he said.

'No!' I said. 'I'm trying to have a quiet wash.'

'It's Christmas!' Gruff said. 'Who needs a wash at Christmas?'

Gruff has no understanding of cleanliness. But then he is just a dog, after all.

He spent the rest of the time till everyone came home, chasing his tail round and round the kitchen. You'd think he'd have worn himself out, but it takes a lot to wear out Gruff. As soon as he gets back from a walk, he's ready to go for another one.

'Sarah, would you mind laying the table?' her mum asks. 'I've put all the cutlery out.'

Sarah's about to pick it up when she says, 'Mum, there's five of everything.'

'That's right,' says her mum.

'But there are only four of us,' says Sarah.

'Are there?' says her mum. 'Oh, well. Put the spare ones out anyway.'

Sarah frowns. She looks at her dad. He shrugs at her. She looks at me. I am unable to shrug but I put my head on one side to try to show that I am being supportive in her confusion.

'But that's silly,' says Sarah. 'Have you invited someone for Christmas lunch and not told me?'

Hardly are the words out of her mouth, when John walks in through the front door with Gruff (who's still behaving as though he hasn't had a walk in a month).

'I'm back!' John calls.

He stands in the kitchen doorway. 'Lunch smells great,' he says. 'I'm starving.'

We all look up at him. He's grinning all over his face.

'John, why are you grinning like that?' Sarah asks.

'It's Christmas!' answers John. 'And, erm ... there's sort of a surprise.'

John steps to one side to make room in the doorway.

And there's someone else there.

It's Mrs Allbright!

'Hello!' says Sarah's mum cheerfully. 'Sarah's just laying the table. Make yourself at home. Lunch won't be long.'

Sarah's mouth falls open. She gasps the loudest gasp I've ever heard! For a moment I'm not sure if she's happy about this new development or not.

'Happy Christmas, Sarah!' says Mrs Allbright.

'But … ' Sarah doesn't seem to know how to answer. 'I didn't know you were coming for lunch,' she gulps.

'Well,' smiles Mrs Allbright, 'we thought we'd keep it as a surprise. John popped in yesterday evening. He said you were a little upset over a mix-up with some party invitation and to make things better, would I come over today and share a bit of Christmas with you.'

'Did he?' Sarah says.

'So I said,' continues Mrs Allbright, '"There's nothing I'd like better. To be honest with you, John," I said, "I'd absolutely love it." And here I am. I hope that's all right with you, Sarah?'

Sarah looks at her mum and dad. She looks at John. She puts down the knives and forks she's holding and gives Mrs Allbright a huge hug.

'I'm so sorry, Mrs Allbright,' she begins. 'I had your invitation and I …'

'It doesn't matter, dear,' Mrs Allbright says. She has such a kind voice. 'The ins and the outs aren't important. Just don't you worry anymore.'

You know, sometimes humans can be very frustrating. Just when you think you're getting to the bottom of something, they spoil it all by saying, 'The ins and the outs aren't important'. Of course they're important! If I knew the ins and the outs, then I'd understand them! As it is, I'm still completely in the dark and probably always will be.

But then again, perhaps Mrs Allbright's right. Perhaps the ins and the outs don't matter as long as everyone's happy again.

Sarah's laying the table now and she's beaming all over her face.

And that sad look I've been seeing in her eyes? I'm very pleased to say it's completely vanished.

Evening

I've been for a prowl around the garden. It's dark now, very still outside. No one about. Barely even a car driving down the road. The air's chilly so I don't stay out long.

Gruff's waiting for me as I slip back inside through the cat flap. He barks, trying to make me jump.

I don't.

'You'll have to find a new trick,' I say. 'You've done that one so many times, it doesn't work anymore.'

'Mrs Allbright's still here,' says Gruff.

'That's nice,' I say. 'I get the feeling Sarah didn't want her to be on her own today.'

Gruff looks impressed. 'How did you know that?' he asks.

I sit on the floor and give myself a bit of a spruce up.

'Just something in Sarah's eyes,' I say.

'You're right,' says Gruff. 'Sarah said to John that the best thing about this Christmas Day has been making room in the stable for Mrs Allbright after all.'

'Did she really?' I say.

'Yes, really!' says Gruff. 'Only … I didn't know we had a stable.'

I stand up and stretch. 'Don't worry about it,' I say. 'I'll explain later.'

We wander into the lounge. It's cosy and bright and the lights on the Christmas tree twinkle. Our five people are watching television. Sarah and John sit either side of Mrs Allbright on the sofa and Gruff makes himself comfy on top of John's feet.

I like it that Sarah and John are friends again. They've been through a bit of a dark time lately with all their arguing. But, as He always does when you ask Him to, God seems to have worked things out and chased the shadows away.

I rather like having a guest for Christmas, too. As far as I'm concerned, you can never have too many laps to snuggle into.

Now … which one shall I choose?

Topz SECRET STORIES!

The *Topz Secret Stories* are full of fun and they also help you to discover how God is always with us through good and bad times. Find out how The Topz Gang and the Dixons Gang can learn from each other in these action-packed stories.

Danny and the Runaway
ISBN: 978-1-85345-991-7

The Cloudgate Mystery
ISBN: 978-1-85345-992-4

One Too Many for Benny
ISBN: 978-1-85345-915-3

Pantomime Pandemonium
ISBN: 978-1-85345-916-0

Dixons' Den
ISBN: 978-1-85345-690-9

Dixons and the Wolf
ISBN: 978-1-85345-691-6

For current prices or to purchase any of the above titles go to **www.cwr.org.uk/store** call 01252 784700 or visit a Christian bookshop.